Desert
Dinosaurs

Desert
Dinosaurs

Anthony D. Fredericks

Countryman Press
Woodstock, Vermont

Interior photographs by the author unless otherwise specified

Map by Paul Woodward, © The Countryman Press

Book design and composition by Caroline Rufo

Desert Dinosaurs

978-0-88150-998-4

Published by The Countryman Press, P.O. Box 748, Woodstock, VT 05091

Distributed by W. W. Norton & Company, Inc., 500 Fifth Avenue, New York, NY 10110

Printed in the United States of America

10 9 8 7 6 5 4 3 2 1

For R.J., Dawn, Marissa, and Alyssa—my favorite Southwestern family!

Desert Dinosaur Destinations

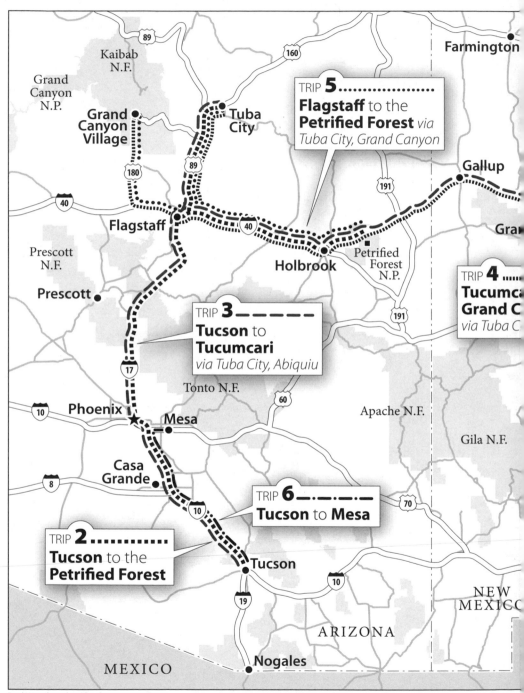

TRIP 5 ....
Flagstaff to the
Petrified Forest *via Tuba City, Grand Canyon*

TRIP 3 — — — —
Tucson to
Tucumcari
via Tuba City, Abiquiu

TRIP 4 .....
Tucumc
Grand C
via Tuba C

TRIP 6 —·—·—·—
Tucson to **Mesa**

TRIP 2 ············
Tucson to the
Petrified Forest

Grand Canyon N.P.
Kaibab N.F.
Grand Canyon Village
Tuba City
Farmington
Gallup
Gra
Flagstaff
Prescott N.F.
Prescott
Holbrook
Petrified Forest N.P.
Tonto N.F.
Phoenix
Mesa
Apache N.F.
Gila N.F.
Casa Grande
Tucson
Nogales

ARIZONA
NEW MEXICO
MEXICO

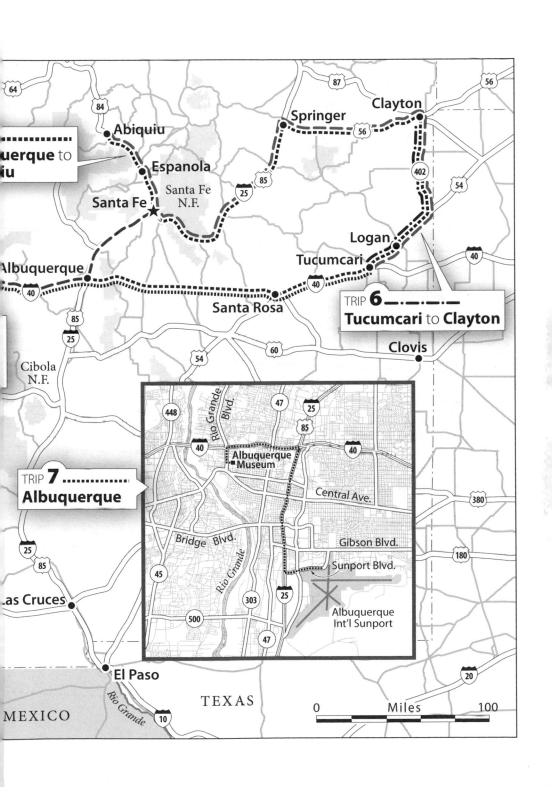

64

84

Abiquiu

erque to
iu

Espanola

Santa Fe
N.F.

Santa Fe

Albuquerque

85

25

Cibola
N.F.

87

Springer

Clayton

56

402

54

85

25

Logan

Tucumcari

40

Santa Rosa

TRIP **6**
Tucumcari to **Clayton**

40

Clovis

54

60

56

TRIP **7**
Albuquerque

448

Rio Grande Blvd.

47

25

85

40

Albuquerque
Museum

40

Central Ave.

380

Bridge Blvd.

Rio Grande

Gibson Blvd.

180

45

Sunport Blvd.

25

303

500

Albuquerque
Int'l Sunport

47

25

85

as Cruces

20

El Paso

10

TEXAS

MEXICO

Rio Grande

0   Miles   100

CONTENTS

III. ON THE ROAD

INTRODUCTION

"Dinosaurs in the desert? No way!"

Dinosaurs in the desert? Absolutely!

It was inevitable!

During the writing of this book I would sometimes find myself
engaged in informal conversations at a local community event, on a
long-distance airplane flight, or at some family holiday celebration.
When the discussants and I had exhausted all the usual conversational
topics (e.g., politics, religion, sex), someone would inquire about my
latest literary venture. When I responded I was researching a book
about dinosaurs in the Southwest, a blanket of silence would quickly
settle over the group, numerous eyebrows would be knitted, and several

mouths would form that characteristic upside-down U—an indication that something was, most likely, amiss (intellectually speaking). Then, some brave soul would pose the obvious, "Dinosaurs in the desert? No way! All the pictures I've seen of dinosaurs show them in lush tropical environments with swamps and palm trees and all those other leafy plants you always see in the lobbies of Miami Beach hotels." And, then, with a somewhat defiant note of assurance (usually fortified by a second or third martini), the expert would emphatically state, "There aren't any dinosaurs in the desert!"

"Well, you see, they really didn't live in the same kind of geographical or climatological places we have today," I would reply with (hopefully) some degree of professorial authority. Of course, then I would have to describe how the geography and climate of Arizona and New Mexico today is somewhat different to what dinosaurs experienced when they were bumping around the Mesozoic landscape for about 165 million years.

But perhaps I'm getting ahead of myself.

It is certain most folks know a little something about dinosaurs. Recently, I asked a group of relatives at a family gathering to share some of their knowledge about dinosaurs. Here is a little of what I got:

- ▶ "Dinosaurs were prehistoric creatures—some were meat eaters, some were plant eaters."
- ▶ "Dinosaurs were very large animals that are no more."
- ▶ "Dinosaurs are extinct reptiles that lived in tropical areas of the world."
- ▶ "A dinosaur is an animal like Godzilla that died millions of years ago. My kids love 'em!"

- ▶ "I believe dinosaurs are dead animals from a long time ago. They were very big and lived in swampy areas with lots of trees and bushes"

- ▶ "Dinosaurs are all about dead reptiles and other prehistoric stuff."

- ▶ "I don't know for sure. I only know what I saw in *Jurassic Park*."

I think it's safe to say that most people have some conventional perceptions (and even misperceptions) about dinosaurs and the environments in which they lived. Either that, or I just have a really strange set of relatives!

What is most certain is many people have the (very common) idea that dinosaurs frequented large swampy areas or lush tropical landscapes. Over the years, this view of dinosaur environments has been perpetuated by scores of children's books, dozens of movies with prehistoric themes,[1] and enormous murals rimming the edges of natural history museums throughout the country.

Allosaurus—a popular Jurassic dinosaur

1 One of my favorite "prehistoric" movies is the film *When Dinosaurs Ruled the Earth* (1970). Its poster proclaimed, "Enter an age of unknown terrors, pagan worship and virgin sacrifice . . ." and featured a scantily clad maiden (a pagan, no doubt) in the jaws of a *T. rex*.

One of the most iconic museum paintings is *The Age of Reptiles*, which occupies the full length of the east wall of the Yale Peabody Museum's Great Hall. The mural is one of the largest in the world, measuring 110 by 16 feet, and required more than 4 1/2 years (1943–47) to complete. Painted by Rudolph Zallinger, the mural showcases a panorama of the evolutionary history of the Earth—from the Devonian period (362 million years ago) to the Cretaceous period (65 million years ago)—based on the best scientific knowledge available at the time. The chronology reads from right to left and portrays prehistoric plants and animals in seemingly natural, realistic landscapes. It has been duplicated in science textbooks, posters, banners, book illustrations, and artistic displays for several decades. At least two-thirds of the mural depicts dinosaurs in tropical or semitropical environments with an abundance of lush vegetation, vast aquatic ecosystems, or incredibly fertile ecological niches. It is a vision many people have whenever they think about prehistoric times.

Pick up any popular dinosaur book—for adults or children—and you will undoubtedly discover similar illustrations, drawings, or depictions of dinosaurs in verdant and leafy landscapes. Popular movies such as *Jurassic Park* perpetuate this vision with resplendent tropical scenes. It almost seems de rigueur for artists or movie producers to place prehistoric reptiles in rich ecosystems—akin, I suppose, to placing certain spoiled divas in sunglasses and expensive sports cars. I guess dinosaurs plus lush environments would be the scientific equivalent of peanut butter and jelly, Mick Jagger and the Rolling Stones, or commercial airlines and nonexistent customer service—in other words, you can't think of one without the other.

As we'll discover in chapter 3, dinosaurs existed for about 165 million years—from approximately 230 million years ago to around 65 million years ago. While that may seem like a very long time for humans, it actually represents only about 3.6 percent of the time the Earth has been in existence. None of the known dinosaur species existed for the entire

165 million years. While some dinosaur species were evolving, some diverged and gave rise to other species, and others were going extinct. A mass extinction event at the end of the Mesozoic era (an asteroid about 6 miles across, slamming into the Earth off the Yucatán coast, seems to be the most likely culprit) effectively brought to a close the reign of dinosaurs.

There is no consensus among paleontologists on the exact number of dinosaur species. Estimates range from around 300 up to 800. According to two researchers at the University of Pennsylvania (who used a well-established mathematical model), we have found only about one-third of all possible species, with a further 1,300 or so still waiting to be discovered.

Scientists divide the Mesozoic era into three periods—the Triassic,

Today's Southwestern environment is very different than it was 65 million years ago.

the Jurassic, and the Cretaceous. The Triassic was a world dominated by terrestrial plants and animals. In the previous three billion years of evolution, animal life was restricted to expansive oceans. Land in what is now New Mexico, Arizona, and much of the Southwest was, for most of this time, an immense floodplain. However, during the Triassic, there was a diversity of animals—everything from large and small reptiles to tiny mammals. A variety of marine organisms lived in the shallow coastal waters along with the last of the large amphibians—the metoposaurs.

The Jurassic period began approximately 199 million years ago. Over the next 60 million years, the combined continents (known as Pangaea) were breaking apart and what we now know as North America drifted northward—away from the equator. What is now the Southwest was dramatically changing. The land was quite similar to a very large desert—with long oceans of sand blanketing the landscape. Much of this land was to eventually change into sandstone cliffs and myriad dunes. The record of the Southwestern plants or animals that lived in this great sea of sand is scant—many of their fossils have disappeared. There is some evidence, however, that dinosaurs and giant marine reptiles were the predominant species.

Then, during the Cretaceous period (which began about 145 million years ago), the climate of the world changed. Because of extensive shallow seas and the positions of the still-moving continental plates, warm waters (shallow water absorbs the sun's heat more readily than deep water) were able to freely circulate throughout the world. This resulted in warmer temperatures—so much so that polar ice caps did not exist and a few species of dinosaurs lived above what is now the Arctic Circle.

About 100 million years ago, an enormous seaway extended from the Gulf of Mexico through Canada to the Arctic Ocean. This sea also covered parts of New Mexico and Arizona. Over the millennia, this seaway advanced and retreated and the shoreline ebbed and flowed across parts of the Southwest in a northwest-to-southeast direction.

Then, near the end of the Cretaceous period, what we now know as the Rocky Mountains was born. The slow rise of this mountain range moved the seas and radically altered the prehistoric landscape. Dinosaur tracks in northeastern Arizona (Tuba City), northern New Mexico (Clayton, Cimarron), and eastern Colorado (Morrison, La Junta) are evidence that dinosaurs, both large and small, roamed freely through the Southwest.

▲▼▲▼▲

This book is a guide to those Southwestern dinosaurs—a way for you to don a pith helmet, grab an imaginary shovel, and set out across Arizona and New Mexico as an amateur paleontologist. If you have some kids along—so much the better. This book will provide the family with some incredible sights—sights you won't find in library books or out-of-date textbooks. In fact, this book is an opportunity to take a trip, not just across a spectacular landscape, but also across time. You'll walk where dinosaurs walked, you'll gaze at skeletons and fossils of some of the most incredible beasts of all time, and you'll learn something about a land and a time that is more spectacular than might appear in any other journey through this region.

This book is also a record of one author's ventures across the sienna-tinged plains, fault-blocked mountains, visually rich topography, stunning visual panoramas, and red-rock outposts of Arizona and New Mexico; in short, a journey of both discovery and desire. I not only sought to learn about a group of long-dead animals that once inhabited what is now the American Southwest, I also wanted to capture the stories surrounding their existence and extinction. I generated questions, read shelves of books, interviewed scientists of every stripe, and traveled serpentine back roads and 75 mph straight-as-an-arrow highways in an exploration of both past and present. I was seeking both fossils and facts in a land of incomparable horizons, evolving landscapes, and prehistoric secrets.

So, dinosaurs in the desert?

Absolutely!

Yes, it does get hot but, hey, look at these views!

I. WHAT YOU NEED TO KNOW

Chapter 1

Your Southwestern Course Schedule

The Great Plains (eastern New Mexico)

The Southwest is like no other region of the United States—it is diverse, majestic, panoramic, and, well, incredible! One day, you might hear the howl of a coyote in a distant canyon beyond an Arizona campground; the following, you might stand on the rim of the greatest natural wonder in the world frantically taking photos; the next, you might be lunching on the world's most incredible tacos in the small town of Española,

Lower Cliff Dwelling, Tonto National Monument, Roosevelt, AZ

New Mexico; and the following, you might be tracking million-year-old sets of dinosaur prints outside the tiny northeastern New Mexico town of Clayton. This is a land without equal; a land that will draw you in, delight your senses, and never let you go . . . no matter where you live or what language you speak. It is a land of both intrigue and mystery, a land ripe for exploration.

You are here because of some prehistoric beasts. You are here because you want to learn more about them, seek the places where they lived and died and perhaps even walk in their footprints or hold a piece of their skeleton in your hands. Indeed, you have come to the right place—a place that will fill your camera as much as it will fill your soul. Your memories of the incredible vistas, flashing sunsets, and majestic landscapes will be recorded both digitally as well as spiritually.

But before you begin your dinosaurian discoveries, I thought it might be a good idea if you learn just a tad about this place of magic. And so,

Colorado Plateau (approximate area)

as every good professor would do, I have put together several courses for your "first semester" in the Southwest. I have intentionally kept these courses short and have waived all written assignments, midterm exams, and internships. My intent is not to inundate you with lots of information; rather, to give you little slices of larger courses that will pique your interest, stimulate your desire to examine the Southwest in much greater detail, and hopefully, dial up your imagination to the nth degree!

Welcome to Southwestology 101!

GEOLOGY

Ask people across the country to name the most incredible geologic wonder in the entire Southwest and 99.99 percent of them will tell you it's the Grand Canyon (the other 0.01 percent were probably too busy texting their roommates during their "Introduction to Geology" course to remember). To say that the Grand Canyon is majestic is to understate the obvious. It's fabulous!

GRAND CANYON

- ▶ The Grand Canyon is 277 miles long.
- ▶ It has an average width of 10 miles.
- ▶ Its widest point is 18 miles across.
- ▶ Its narrowest point is 600 feet (Marble Canyon)
- ▶ The Colorado River, which flows west through the canyon, averages 300 feet in width, 40 feet in depth, and flows at an average speed of 4 miles per hour.
- ▶ There are 160 rapids in the canyon (70 are considered major).
- ▶ The canyon has approximately 70 species of mammals, 250 species of birds, 25 types of reptiles, and 5 species of amphibians.
- ▶ There are more than 1,500 species of plants in the canyon.
- ▶ There are 400 miles of trails.
- ▶ There are 2,700 archaeological sites within the park.
- ▶ 4.5 million people visit the Grand Canyon every year.

Southwestern geology is both dramatic and dynamic!

To many geologists, the Grand Canyon is two stories in one. The first story has to do with how the canyon was created in the first place. It seems that about 65 to 70 million years ago, sections of the Earth's surface began a general uplift. It has been speculated that the land we now know as the Colorado Plateau rose approximately 5,000 to 10,000 feet. As a result of higher elevation, the steepness, or gradient, of the Colorado River also rose. The speed of the water rushing down the Colorado River increased, and cut more effectively through the surrounding rock. Increased rainfall through this period also added to the river's powers of erosion.

The second part of the story is equally compelling—that is, how old the Grand Canyon is. Its age will depend on who you are talking to or what you are reading. In short, there is no general consensus. Most geological estimates place the age of the canyon at about 5 to 6 million years. However, a study published in 2008 reported on uranium-lead dating that suggested the canyon originated considerably earlier—17 million years ago. Despite the nonagreement on the age of the canyon, here is what we can agree on: the Grand Canyon is relatively young—at least in geological terms.

Did dinosaurs inhabit the area we now know as the Grand Canyon? We don't know! Although the Grand Canyon area was once part of one or more shallow seas in prehistoric times, and dinosaurs frequently inhabited the shorelines of shallow seas, we're not certain if any of these prehistoric beasts inhabited this area specifically. That's simply because we haven't discovered any body fossils in or around the Grand Canyon area. Who knows, maybe you or your kids might be the first (think: *early retirement* or *college scholarship*).

Southwestern Geology

Many people are surprised to learn that what we now call the Southwest was once an area that was washed by great and shallow seas—enormous tracts of water that advanced and retreated over the landscape for hundreds of millions of years. The region was also subject to great

The Wave, a sandstone formation in northern Arizona

geological events—the initial rise, eventual decline, and ultimate
elevation of mountain ranges (such as the Rocky Mountains) along
with a great movement of continents that migrated across the globe.
Weathering and erosion were also constant factors in shaping the
land—a multimillion year "sandpapering" project that significantly
altered the land and shaped its ever-evolving features.

For long periods of time, much of the area we now call the Southwest
may have resembled several of today's Middle Eastern countries: Large
floodplains and enormous deltas were prominent geographic features.
Great deserts spread out in various directions, punctuated by large sand
dunes and windswept mountains. Much of this prehistoric geology has
been preserved in the form of vast sandstone deposits throughout the
region.

Then, in a most dramatic fashion, what we now know as North
America began sliding westward over a piece of the Earth's crust known
as the East Pacific Plate. This resulted in a momentous separation from
Europe and left behind a very large and very gaping expanse we now call

the Atlantic Ocean. This event is known by geologists as the Laramide orogeny—a slowly evolving geological occurrence that created the modern-day Rocky Mountains and uplifted what we call the Colorado Plateau. Starting in the Late Cretaceous period, 70 to 80 million years ago, and ending about 35 to 55 million years ago, this action eventually transformed the Southwest from a coastal area into a vast interior region. This period was named for the Laramie Mountains of eastern Wyoming. (An orogeny is a process of mountain formation, especially a folding of the Earth's crust.)

Other geological forces were also at work to shape the landscape. About 30 million years ago, parts of the Earth began a slow and steady "stretching" in an east–west direction. The land, particularly in New Mexico and Texas, cracked along several fault zones. It was through one of these zones that a rift valley was created—this valley is where New Mexico's Rio Grande now flows. These same forces were also at work helping to create the stepped plateau of northern Arizona.

Somewhere between 9 and 14 million years ago, a large region of north–south cracks began to appear in what is now western Utah,

Arizona, and Nevada. This area is often referred to as the Basin and Range Province (see "Geography"). These cracks resulted in hundreds of miles of valleys and mountain ranges that eventually filled the region between the Sierra Nevada and the Rocky Mountains.

Although the Earth was engaged in various periods of stretching, straining, faulting and moving over the millennia, it would be safe to say that the most dramatic geological shaping of the Southwest was due to external factors. Erosion and weathering have done more to shape this environment than we might imagine. Consider this: Pounding rainstorms (over millions of years) ripped through soft sedimentary rocks, carving an incredible variety of geological features. Wild, whipping winds (again, over many millions of years) scraped and shaped the landscape into arches, buttes, mesas, and long flatlands. Rivers ran swiftly through the landscape, carving and sculpting the land into dozens of iconic features. In short, this is a land that was—and still is—dominated as much by the external forces of nature as it was by ancient subterranean events.

Southwestern geography is always spectacular!

GEOGRAPHY

Arizona

Most people have the mistaken impression that Arizona is nothing
more than one big desert. Not so! In reality, more than half the state
consists of mountain and plateau areas. Most geographers divide
Arizona into three major land areas: the Colorado Plateau, the
Transition Zone, and the Basin and Ridge Region.

The Colorado Plateau This section of Arizona, which has mostly
flat, level land as well as a few soaring mountains and long canyons,
encompasses the northern two-fifths of the state. Besides the Grand
Canyon, two other equally dramatic canyons emblematic of this
region include Canyon de Chelly (one of my favorites) and the always
photogenic Oak Creek Canyon (a place where your senses will go on
visual overload . . . and probably never recover!). Many of the mountains
are forested, but there are also significant areas of dry desert.

Prominent geographical features in this section include the visually
stunning Monument Valley (if you've seen any John Wayne movies,

you'll definitely recognize this part of the Southwest). The Painted Desert and the Petrified Forest (which we'll visit later in this book) are also dramatic features of this area. The southern edge of the Colorado Plateau is bordered by the Mogollon Rim that runs from central Arizona through to New Mexico.

The Transition Zone This thin strip of land lies just to the south of the Colorado Plateau. Much of the landscape features a rugged series of mountain ranges and valleys. These include the White Mountains, Santa Maria Mountains, and the Cornell Mountains.

The Basin and Ridge Province This large section of Arizona, predominantly in the south, features several mountain ranges running from the northwest in a southeasterly direction. These ranges include such notables as the dramatic Chiricahuas, the Gila Mountains in Yuma County, the Huachuca Mountains southeast of Tucson, and the always enigmatic Superstition Mountains. This is also a significant fruit and vegetables farming region for the state, with everything from apples to zucchini.

The Hopi House near the Grand Canyon is part of Arizona's rich history.

Whatever you do, don't miss Monument Valley!

FAST FACTS
ARIZONA GEOGRAPHY

- ▶ **Length x Width:** 400 miles long by 310 miles wide
- ▶ **Total Area:** 114,006 square miles (sixth-largest state)
- ▶ **Highest Point:** Humphreys Peak (12,633 feet)
- ▶ **Lowest Point:** Colorado River (70 feet)
- ▶ **Mean Elevation:** 4,100 feet above sea level

New Mexico

Just like its neighbor, New Mexico is often divided into three primary geographical zones.

The Great Plains Most of the eastern third of the state is covered by the Great Plains—an enormous expanse of land in the middle of the country. This part of New Mexico includes plateaus in the north and wide, open spaces southward toward the Pecos River. Scattered throughout this region are deep canyons that have been cut into the landscape by long, winding rivers. Sheep and cattle ranchers take advantage of the grassy lands to the north, while the southern regions feature farming and agricultural products. The High Plains or Staked Plains (Llano Estacado), a significant portion of eastern New Mexico, ranges in elevation from 3,000 to 5,000 feet.

The views—up or down—are incredible!

The Central Mountains Many readers might be surprised to learn that New Mexico is one of the Rocky Mountain states. That mountain range enters the state in the north (from Colorado) and extends down to the Rio Grande (as it becomes the border with Texas) in the south. A significant length of the river runs through the Rockies from north to south. Part of the Rockies is the always dramatic Sangre de Cristo (Blood of Christ) Mountains. One story has it that the mountains got their name from the crimson colors that echo off them during sunsets and sunrises. The Rio Grande Valley, one of the richest agricultural regions in the state, has vast acres of very productive farmland.

The Basin and Range Province This section encompasses about one-third of the state and lies to the south of the Rocky Mountain Region. It extends south from around Santa Fe to Mexico and west to Arizona. Much of this area is comprised of rugged mountain ranges, such as the Guadalupe, Sacramento, and San Andres Ranges. To the south are long flatlands and a host of classic western towns.

FAST FACTS

NEW MEXICO GEOGRAPHY

- ▶ **Length x Width:** 370 miles long by 343 miles wide
- ▶ **Total Area:** 121,598 square miles (fifth-largest state)
- ▶ **Highest Point:** Wheeler Peak (13,161 feet)
- ▶ **Lowest Point:** Red Bluff Reservoir (2,842 feet)
- ▶ **Mean Elevation:** 5,700 feet above sea level

ARCHAEOLOGY

If you're looking for an archaeological treasure trove, then you've come to the right place. You can spend years (perhaps even decades) exploring all the archaeology of the Southwest and never see all of it. This is a land of many mysteries: Civilizations have risen, then disappeared—virtually into thin air. Strange drawings, mysterious etchings, and enigmatic petroglyphs (4,000 years old) have been squiggled onto tall rocks and vast canyon walls. And magnificent agricultural systems and equally magnificent irrigation canals have been created, rivaling anything found in distant European capitals.

Long after dinosaurs and other prehistoric beasts left their footprints on this ancient land, humans arrived. Although there is much debate

Ancestral Puebloan ruins at Canyon de Chelly, Arizona

and much controversy over when this occurred, it is generally agreed that the first peoples in this area settled near what is now Clovis, New Mexico, about 11,000 years ago. Spear points embedded in the bones of several large mammoths led archaeologists to determine that these first peoples were initially hunters. Several archaeologists estimate that the production of the Clovis points lasted for approximately 200 years. This seems to suggest that wildlife in the area was eradicated very quickly

and that these people may have been compelled to supplement their diet with fruits, berries, seeds, and roots. As a result, people who were once hunters may have become hunter-gatherers.

The period from about 6500 to 1200 BC is known as the Desert Archaic period (older texts refer to this as Basketmaker I—a term no longer used). This term focuses mainly on those people—most often bands of hunter-gatherers—who foraged through the wilderness. Some archaeological artifacts suggest that several of these tribes may have engaged in spear hunting as an alternate way to secure their food. However, climatic conditions during this time period—significant periods of drought—may have had an adverse effect on animal life, and ultimately, on the tribes' ability to hunt those animals.

From about 1200 BC to AD 50 (the Late Desert Archaic period) paleo-Indians in the region began using caves as living quarters on a seasonal basis. Many of those caves were adorned with various types of rock art—a permanent record of the

White House ruins in Canyon de Chelly National Monument

customs, environment, and animals of the time. Although archaeologists are still debating the function and reason for rock art (e.g., religious, medicinal, or ceremonial), it remains as an enduring legacy of nearly every known ancestral people in the region. Several archaeological ruins show that corn and squash were grown at this time.

Three dominant cultures were then firmly in place throughout the Southwest. These included the Ancestral Pueblans (formerly known as the Anasazi), the Mogollon of the central mountains and valleys, and the Hohokam of the desert regions.

The Ancestral Pueblans inhabited the land in and around the Colorado Plateau (which today we refer to as the Four Corners region because it is the only place in the United States where four states—northeastern Arizona, northwestern New Mexico, Southwestern Colorado, and southeastern Utah—share a common point[2]). The Ancestral Pueblans left some of the richest archaeological sites and ancient settlements ever known. If you visit this region, I heartedly suggest a journey to the Navajo National Monument and Canyon de Chelly National Monument in Arizona, or to Bandelier National Monument, Aztec Ruins National Monument, and Chaco Culture National Historical Park in New Mexico. They are truly sights to behold!

From approximately 200 BC to about AD 1400, the Mogollon culture was firmly established near what is now the Mexican border. These peoples lived in small communities that were often perched on isolated mesas or ridge tops. Their existence was primarily agricultural, although as time went on they depended more and more on hunting and foraging for food. One of the most recognizable features of the Mogollon culture was the kiva—a circular, underground chamber used for special ceremonies.

From about 300 BC to AD 1400, the Hohokam had a flourishing presence in the wide deserts of Arizona. They were able to adapt to desert life by creating an incredible river-fed irrigation system that

---

2 If you visit, be sure to get the classic photo of a family member with at least one body part—hands and feet are suggested—placed in each of the four states.

involved hundreds of miles of canals (the remains of these irrigation canals now lie under the streets of Phoenix). They also developed low, earthen pyramids (perhaps serving as temples) and sunken ball courts. Archaeologists have discovered numerous examples of intricately detailed pottery attesting to their artistry.

In one of the Southwest's constantly enduring mysteries, the Hohokam mysteriously disappeared sometime around 1400. They abandoned their villages, left their fertile fields, and left for . . . ? There are several theories for this flight—most likely involving a combination of factors, including drought, overhunting, group conflict, and disease.

MORE GREAT BOOKS AND STUFF

For a more thorough description of the peoples and times of this region, you may want to obtain one of the following books—each of which will dazzle you with amazing stories and equally amazing prehistory:

▶ Childs, Craig. *House of Rain: Tracking a Vanished Civilization Across the American Southwest* (New York, NY: Back Bay Books, 2008).

▶ Kantner, John. *Ancient Puebloan Southwest* (New York, NY: Cambridge University Press, 2004).

▶ Noble, David Grant. *Ancient Ruins of the Southwest: An Archaeological Guide* (New York, NY: Cooper Square Publishing, 2000).

▶ Roberts, David. *In Search of the Old Ones* (New York, NY: Simon and Schuster, 1997). [Packed with dynamic writing, this is my personal favorite.]

Significant Events in Arizona History

1539 Father Marcos de Niza, in his search for cities of gold, explores Arizona and claims it for Spain.

1752 After many revolts from the Pima and Papago tribes, the first permanent settlement was established in Tubac.

● 1600   ● 1700

1540 Francisco Vasquez de Coronado of Spain searches for the mysterious Seven Cities of Cibola. He doesn't find the cities (supposedly constructed of gold), but claims Arizona as part of New Spain.

Significant Events in New Mexico History

1536 Cabeza de Vaca, Estevan the Moor and two others cross what is now southern New Mexico.

1626 The infamous Spanish Inquisition was established in New Mexico.

1692 Don Diego de Vargas proclaimed a formal act of possession and recolonizes Santa Fe.

● 1600   ● 1700

1598 Juan de Onate establishes the first Spanish capital of San Juan de los Caballeros at the Tewa village of Ohke north of present-day Española.

1706 Villa de Albuquerque is founded.

1848 The United States won the Mexican War and eventually gained all of Arizona north of the Gila River.

1867 The capital was changed to Tucson. Eventually it was moved to Phoenix in 1889.

1912 February 14th: Arizona becomes the 48th State. The first governor is George W. P. Hunt.

● 1800   ● 1900   ● 2000

1863 The territory of Arizona is created by the U.S. Congress, with Prescott as capital.

1881 On October 26 Wyatt Earp and three of his brothers, together with Doc Holliday, cemented their place in western lore during the gunfight at the O.K. Corral.

1968 London Bridge (which had been falling down for some time) is moved — block by block — to Lake Havasu City, Arizona.

1846 The Mexican-American War begins. New Mexico is annexed to the United States.

1881 Billy the Kid is shot by Sheriff Pat Garrett in Fort Sumner, NM.

1945 The world's first atomic bomb is detonated at Trinity Site in southern New Mexico.

● 1800   ● 1900   ● 2000

1854 The Gadsden Purchase (from Mexico) adds 45,000 square miles to the New Mexico territory.

1912 January 6: New Mexico is admitted to the Union as the 47th state. William C. McDonald is the first governor.

1998 New Mexico celebrates its cuartocentenario — its 400th anniversary commemorating its 1598 founding by Juan de Onate.

BIOLOGY

Animals

Say the word *desert* and, for most people, the first animal that comes
to mind will be a rattlesnake. However, those same individuals are
surprised to learn that deserts have an amazing and eclectic variety of
animals—many of which are seemingly hidden away as (human) visitors
speed across the Southwest in their air-conditioned vehicles. Many
desert animals are nocturnal—sleeping during the day and out hunting
during the night—a time, by the way, when most (human) visitors are
more interested in sampling beverages with salted rims and slices of
lime, instead of looking for wildlife.

The following list is a much abbreviated collection of Southwestern
wildlife. Because this book is focused more on the wildlife that
was around millions of years ago instead of what roams this region
today, you are encouraged to seek other books (or websites) for more
information about the denizens of the desert.

Rattlesnake There are 10 species of rattlesnakes in Arizona.
Rattlesnakes belong to a group of poisonous snakes known as pit vipers.
These snakes have small depressions, or pits, on both sides of their face.
These pits are used as temperature detectors to help them locate prey in
the dark.[3]

Scorpion There are more than 1,300 species of scorpions worldwide.
Although some species have as many as twelve eyes, scorpions have very
poor eyesight. They have sense organs on their belly to detect chemical
trails of their own species.[4]

Gila Monster These characteristic desert creatures are named for the

---

3   From 6 feet away, a rattlesnake is able to detect a 0.009°F rise in the temperature of an approaching animal.

4   Scorpions will fluoresce (glow) under a black light. Several companies (including
Amazon. com) sell ultraviolet LED flashlights (Scorpion Master is one brand name)
to assist you in locating scorpions in your shoes, your clothing, or under your hotel
room bed!).

Gila monster

Gila River Basin in Arizona. Their relatives go back nearly 50 million years. They have a poisonous bite; however, they are not aggressive toward humans. These animals, along with the Mexican beaded lizard, are the only two poisonous lizards in the world.

Kangaroo Rat This animal's name comes from the fact that it hops over the ground in much the same way as a kangaroo. Kangaroo rats reach an overall length of 9 to 14 inches (including the tail) and are often pale in color with shades of tan, cream, and off-white.

Elf Owl The elf owl is the world's smallest owl. They typically live in the abandoned nests (in a saguaro cactus) of gila woodpeckers. Typically, their nests are 15 to 35 feet above the ground. They can be easily identified by their high-pitched, squeaky whistle.

Lesser Long-nosed Bat This creature rests in caves during the day and feeds at night. Its eyes are best adapted for seeing in the dark, although it only sees in black and white. It plays a critical role in the pollination of the saguaro cactus—transferring pollen from one flower to another.

Javelina The javelina is the only wild, piglike animal found in the United States. Although they look similar to pigs, javelinas are much smaller. They are most active in the evening and enjoy eating prickly pears because of the fruit's high water content. Javelinas have good hearing but very poor eyesight.

Coyote Coyotes sometimes come out during the day and at twilight, but are most often seen (and heard) during the night. About the size of a large dog, these familiar desert creatures make howling, yelping, or barking sounds that can be heard for long distances.

Desert Tortoise These slow-moving, prehistoric-looking creatures may live to be well over 100 years old. They like to crawl into burrows to escape the desert heat, but will sometimes come out to look for plants

The always wily coyote!

to eat. A desert tortoise is able to live where the ground temperature reaches 140°F.

Red-tailed Hawk The red-tailed hawk weighs between 2 and 4 pounds. Females are larger than males, with a wingspan up to 56 inches. A soaring red-tail often gives a hoarse scream and will use its sharp eyesight to locate small animals on the ground below.

Painted Lady Butterfly This insect is found throughout the Sonoran Desert. It is light orange in color with white spots and black edges on its wings. Before it can fly, it must warm up in the morning sun. Then it dances through the desert, looking for flowers, especially lupines.

MORE GREAT BOOKS AND STUFF

If you have kids (or grandchildren) you may want to introduce them to two of my children's books—each of which has won multiple awards. These books are designed to provide young readers with information about some of the amazing nocturnal and diurnal wildlife in the Southwestern desert.

▶ *Desert Night Desert Day* (Tucson, AZ: Rio Nuevo Publishers, 2011; Grades K–2).

▶ *Around One Cactus: Owls, Bats and Leaping Rats* (Nevada City, CA: Dawn Publications, 2003; Grades 2–4).

Plants

Most people think of the saguaro (suh-WAR-oh) cactus as the most iconic of all desert plants. Living exclusively in the Sonoran desert, it is recognized around the world. However, it is only one of many plants you'll discover throughout the varied and dynamic Southwest.

Following are just a few of the plants growing in the desert. Take some time (and take some photos) to learn more about desert botany and you will be incredibly impressed.

Saguaro Cactus The saguaro cactus thrives in rocky areas from sea level to 4,500 feet in elevation. It requires very little water and can go

A saguaro cactus standing guard

for two years without rain. Surprisingly, about 75 to 95 percent of the cactus's weight is water. The saguaro doesn't begin to grow "arms" until it is at least 70 years old.

Creosote Bush This common desert plant is most often found in dry valleys at elevations below 3,000 feet. Like the cactus, it is extremely drought resistant with an extensive root system. Its leaves are coated with a resinous substance and for this reason it is often referred to as "greasewood."

Mesquite Mesquite, a small tree that reaches 20 feet in height, can be found throughout the Southwest. There are three varieties: Honey, Screwbean, and Velvet—all of which form bean pods and serve as a valuable food source for many desert animals.

Prickly Pear Cactus Although prickly pears are native to the United States, they are cosmopolitan plants and can be found in many countries throughout South America, Africa, and the Mediterranean. Prickly pears are distinguished by large "pads," colorful blooms, and a very tasty fruit. In some parts of the world, including the United States, they are grown and harvested as a commercial crop.

Tumbleweed One of the most characteristic of all Southwestern plants (they have been featured in scores of Westerns), tumbleweeds look like "botanical skeletons" rolling and bouncing across the ground. These plants may be as small as basketballs or as large as an electric car.

Tumbling tumbleweed

Ponderosa Pine This plant occurs throughout the West—in locations with an average of less than 20 inches of annual precipitation. It can be found on mesas and mountain ranges from 6,000 to 10,000 feet in elevation. Its thick bark is extremely resistant to fire.

Mormon Tea There are five species of Mormon Tea growing in the Southwestern deserts of the United States. Mesas, plains, and sandy soil including dunes below 5,000 feet are its typical environments. All five species have been used for a variety of medicinal purposes by desert peoples over the centuries.

Desert Marigold Long stretches of desert marigolds blooming just after a rainfall is one of the most beautiful of all desert sights. The profusion of golden yellow flowers often attract many insects (along with hordes of photo-snapping tourists). Desert marigolds can be found throughout the Southwest on rocky desert floors, stony slopes, and sandy plains.

Desert marigold

CLIMATOLOGY

There's the saying, "Everybody talks about the weather, but nobody does anything about it." It's true that if this is your first visit to the Southwest, a primary topic of conversation will be the weather—both before your trip begins and long after it is over. If you've never traveled through Arizona or New Mexico you may have some misperceptions and misconceptions about the climate of this region. Let's see if we can shake some of that misinformation loose.

First things first. Yes, it does get hot here. Phoenix consistently ranks as the number one hottest city in the United States. On average, it has 106 days every year in which the daily temperature climbs to 100°F or more. The second-place city—Las Vegas—only gets a measly 72 days a year with temperatures above 100°F. As a result of Phoenix's "hot" reputation, many people assume that the entire Southwest is equally torrid. Well, that's partially true . . . and partially false.

Skiing in Arizona? You bet!

Many people will tell you that Arizona (for example) is a desert. That's true, but only for about 73 percent of the state. The other 27 percent of Arizona is forest. New Mexico, on the other hand, is mostly mountains, high plains, and desert, with a climate that is generally semiarid to arid.

Just for fun, take the border between Arizona and New Mexico and turn it on its side so that it runs horizontally through the middle of the two states. What you have just created are two new territories—for now we'll call them Northern Arizona/New Mexico and Southern Arizona/ New Mexico. What you've also done is broadly created two varied, and quite different, climatic zones.

In Northern Arizona/New Mexico, you'll discover a range of geographic features from high mesas, towering mountains, broad deserts, and that very impressive hole we talked about earlier (the Grand Canyon). In winter it can get chilly (–50°F at Gavilan, New Mexico, on February 1, 1951, and –40°F at Hawley Lake, Arizona, on January 7, 1971), so if you're swinging through this area in January or February, it might be a good idea to toss a jacket (or two) into your suitcase.

You may also want to know that it does snow in the mountains of Northern Arizona/New Mexico, with the mountains of north central New Mexico recording up to 25 feet per year. Ski bums who regularly travel to Taos, New Mexico, and Flagstaff, Arizona, will tell you about the great skiing in these mountains. You'll also discover that the sun is a regular during the winter months—frequently warming the air into the high 50s.

In Southern Arizona/New Mexico, you'll discover a stunning variety of temperatures, depending on the season of the year. Autumn weather is typically sunny and mild, averaging a minimum of 60°F, making this a most pleasant time to visit. November through February are the coldest months, with temperatures typically ranging from 40° to 75°F. About midway through February, the temperatures start to rise again, with warm days and cool breezy nights. The summer months of June through September bring a dry heat ranging from 90° to 128°F.

Arizona has an average annual rainfall of 12.7 inches, which comes during two rainy seasons. Cold fronts usually come in from the Pacific Ocean during the winter months, whereas the end of summer is the infamous monsoon season. New Mexico's average precipitation rate is 13.9 inches. Keep in mind that elevation greatly affects precipitation. Thus, it is not unusual for Southern Arizona/New Mexico to receive as few as 3 inches of rain per year, whereas Northern Arizona/New Mexico might get as many as 300 inches (25 feet) of snowfall in the high mountain areas.

The desert is often hot and dry.

Chapter 2

Your Southwestern Visitor's Guide

A SOUTHWESTERN STATE OF MIND

It was the early 1960s and my parents decided that a few years at a well-regarded college preparatory school would help shape the intellectual possibilities of their young adolescent son. Thus, I had the good fortune to spend five incredible years at the Orme School (www.ormeschool .org)—a nationally recognized prep school situated on a 40,000-acre working cattle ranch in central Arizona. Each of the 150 students at the school was assigned his or her own horse and was charged with the responsibility of caring for said steed. And every fall and spring we would participate in a right-out-of-the-movies authentic cattle roundup—gathering stray cows; branding, inoculating, ear marking

Amateur paleontologists will find much to discover throughout the Southwest.

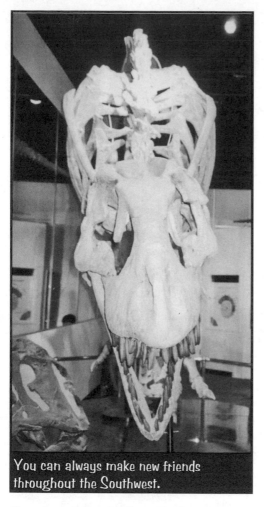
You can always make new friends throughout the Southwest.

new calves; and doing all the other things that cowboys and cowgirls do to their cows. Equally significant were the small classes and dedicated teachers that ensured us an education both rigorous and demanding.

Each spring, the school would close down for ten days or so and we would pile sleeping bags, duffel bags, and ourselves into the back of a half-dozen cattle trucks and tour selected areas of the Southwest. Every other year meant a journey to the Grand Canyon as well as the beautiful Canyon de Chelly in northeastern Arizona. We also visited, among other sites, Zion National Park, the Petrified Forest, Shiprock, Mesa Verde, and the Inter-Tribal Indian Ceremonial at Gallop. Each evening we would unload the trucks, pitch our tents, set up the campsite, eat slightly warmed chili, and sing western ballads around a towering fire. Some years we would even dip below the border to visit the quaint towns and ancient pueblos of Mexico.

Those caravans were always dusty and dirty and the roads were often unpaved. But we saw parts of the world that few tourists visit. We gained both an awareness and an appreciation for the people and the land on which they lived. While visiting Old Oraibi, the oldest continuously occupied (since AD 1150) settlement in North America, we talked with the natives and listened to their stories of the Earth—stories that celebrated their closeness with nature and their oneness with the plants and animals with whom they shared the land. We learned more about the natural world than we could ever find in any textbook. We walked across it, we slept in it, and we occasionally found unintended bits of it in our peanut butter sandwiches, while gazing out across the sun-splashed and prehistoric rock formations of the Grand Canyon.

At the Orme School our adolescent minds were exposed to a side of nature that is often missed by urban dwellers. Whether it was on those extended caravan trips across the long, flat New Mexican desert or a horse ride out through chaparral-choked dry washes and cliffside ravines that rimmed the campus, we developed a familiarity with both the geology and geography of the Southwest. This was a dynamic land—filled with an amazing array of lessons and an incredible collection of life experiences. Perhaps it was the primordial beauty, the solitude of a high and distant mesa, the flash of a solitary roadrunner darting across a dirt road, or the crackle of lightning during an unexpected thunderstorm that captured my mind and imagination. This land was, in so many ways, a singular part of my education—an education that engendered a lifelong appreciation of Southwestern territories and an awareness of their timeless cycles.

After two years of college in California, the draw of the Southwest was too much and I returned to complete my undergraduate degree at the University of Arizona. Long after graduation and well into my adult years, I would consume books, articles, photographs, depictions, descriptions, and essays of every conceivable persuasion to maintain my Southwestern connections. I was delighted to learn that dinosaurs, too, were once frequent inhabitants of the American Southwest—they migrated, they traipsed, they plodded over the Mesozoic landscape that was to eventually become Arizona and New Mexico. Where they walked—millions of years later—I was to grow up, attend school, and develop a lifelong fascination for the red rock canyons of Arizona, the sprawling vistas of the vast Sonoran Desert, the natural beauty of the Navajo nation, the national forests and sand-swept landscapes of New Mexico, and the rich cultural heritage of this incredible and dynamic place.

The Southwestern landscapes I grew up with have left lasting impressions . . . for most of my life! Although I now live in the East, I am forever in love with the Southwest—a land of magic and mystery—a land where prehistoric creatures once roamed and where modern-day discoveries are still to be made. I return often, as will you, to explore, to examine, and to rediscover a passion for an ancient land brimming with wonder and overflowing with possibilities . . . both ancient and new.

GETTING THERE

There are several ways of getting to the Southwest, depending on your itinerary, your available time, and your transportation inclinations. If you're from the East Coast you'll find that distances (say, from convenience store to convenience store; or, if you are traveling with kids, from potty break to potty break) are considerably greater here than would be the case back home. Plan accordingly. I always like to utilize a variety of transportation modes, to see the area from several different perspectives. Here are some options to consider:

The Southwest Chief near the summit of Raton Pass, NM

Air

Most visitors to the Southwest fly into one of two major airports: Phoenix Sky Harbor International Airport (PHX), one of the 15 busiest airports of the world, or Albuquerque's International Sunport Airport (ABQ). Both receive all the major commercial airlines. Each of these two airports also has numerous car rental agencies offering you a set of wheels to begin your Southwestern adventures.

For a little variety (and considerably less congestion) you may want to consider one of the smaller airports in the region. Flying into one of these may place you closer to selected sights and save you considerable driving time during your prehistoric explorations. Consider one of the following:

▶ Bullhead City, AZ (IFP) *Airlines:* Allegiant, Canadian North, Sun Country

▶ Farmington, NM (FMN) *Airline:* Great Lakes

▶ Flagstaff, AZ (FLG) *Airline:* US Airways

▶ Grand Canyon, AZ (GCN) *Airlines:* Grand Canyon, Scenic, Vision

  ▶ Prescott, AZ (PRC) *Airline:* Great Lakes

  ▶ Roswell, NM (ROW) *Airlines:* American, New Mexico

  ▶ Santa Fe, NM (SAF) *Airline:* American

  ▶ Tucson, AZ (TUS) *Airlines:* all major

  ▶ Yuma, AZ (NYL) *Airlines:* United, US Airways

Rail

I'm a big fan of rail travel and use it whenever I can. You get to see the landscape in all its glory and experience travel without having to worry about how much gas costs or listen to the constant query, "Are we there yet?" simply because you are there already. Also, when anybody needs a potty break, it's right there with you. Rail travel is a slower pace of transportation and Amtrak doesn't go everywhere you want to go. But combine rail travel with driving and you'll see the Southwest as few people do—you'll get a better sense of the majesty and enormity of this spectacular region. If you can, make one of the following Amtrak (www. amtrak.com) routes part of your Southwestern ventures:

- ▶ **Southwest Chief** Raton, NM; Las Vegas, NM; Lamy, NM (Santa Fe); Albuquerque, NM; Gallop, NM; Winslow, AZ; Flagstaff, AZ; Williams Junction, AZ; Kingman, AZ

- ▶ **Sunset Limited** Deming, NM; Lordsburg, NM; Benson, AZ; Tucson, AZ; Maricopa, AZ; Yuma, AZ

Auto

To get to most out of the Southwestern dinosaur sites profiled in this book, you will need a car—either the family buggy or a rental car. A car will add to your overall expenses (gasoline, maintenance), but you will be able to travel to places far removed from civilization and see parts of this dynamic landscape you might otherwise miss.

You may want to consider using the family car—depending on where your point of origin is. The advantage is that you are familiar with the

San Francisco Peaks, just north of Flagstaff

car—all its quirks and idiosyncrasies—and have an idea on how it will "behave" on the road. The disadvantage is that you'll be piling on the miles, which may result in some maintenance down the line. (Those visitors traveling in from Honolulu may want to ignore the preceding and read the following section instead.)

GETTING AROUND

If you are flying in, you will probably want a rental car. Be aware that their rates vary widely; plan on shopping around. Here's a little-known tip: Most rental car agencies change their rates several times *a day*—particularly in advance of high-demand functions (e.g., festivals or conventions). Keep checking their websites (several times during the day) and you'll probably see fluctuations.[5]

Keep in mind that car rental rates also vary widely according to the season or time of year. If you are flying into Phoenix, for example, during the winter months (prime tourist season), then car rental rates

5   I always start my search at www.kayak.com or www.carrentals.com to compare the various rates. Then I go directly into each car rental company's website, where I sometimes find even lower rates. I'll do this several times a day for several days (or weeks). It takes time, but I've saved more than $25 a day in car rental fees!

will be at their highest. On the other hand, if you arrive in Phoenix in the middle of July, they'll probably be giving away the cars. If you're flying into Albuquerque in early October, then you can also expect sky-high car rental rates due to the Albuquerque International Balloon Festival. Another tip: Consider flying into one of the smaller airports. It may cost a little bit more in airfare, but you might save a bundle on your car rental rate—particularly if you are planning to stay for a week or more. If your travel plans are flexible, you can save a lot on car rates, provided you do your research.

Best advice: Scout around the various car rental websites—those agencies at the airport and those off-site (frequently cheaper as they don't always add all those extra, often confusing, rental costs such as Vehicle License Cost Recovery Fee [huh?]). With a little bit of patience and a little bit of detective work, you can always secure a good rate. Oh, and don't forget the discounts you can get as a member of AAA.

WHEN TO COME

If you've lived your entire life in New Hampshire and you plan on flying in to Phoenix in the middle of July, there is something you should know—it will be *hot* . . . that's *hot* as in "frying an egg on the sidewalk" *hot*! As I am writing this, it is midsummer and the temperature last Saturday in Phoenix was 118°F. The temperature in Manchester, New Hampshire, on the same day was 73°F. Let's just say that the temperature in Arizona was *brutal*, whereas the temperature in New Hampshire was *comfortable*. You are certainly welcome to visit the Southwest in the middle of the summer, but please know what you are getting yourself into.

That said, there is really no bad time to visit Arizona and New Mexico. My personal preferences are spring and fall, for several reasons. First, the temperature is neither too hot nor too cold. Second, depending on which part of the Southwest you are traveling in, these are often the "shoulder" seasons—the times when you can obtain significant discounts on hotel rates and restaurant fare. Third, and just as important, the tourist traffic is down considerably (with the possible exception of the eastern "snowbirds" flocking to the southern parts of New Mexico and Arizona), making your journey less crowded and more hassle free.

You may find the following chart helpful in planning your Southwestern dinosaur visit:

	Time of Year (season)	What you can anticipate
Arizona	December to May (high season)	You'll discover areas in and around ski resorts to be crowded and lodging rates to be higher. Beyond the ski areas will be lots of wide, open spaces. Daytime temperatures are moderate, but nights can be cold.
	June to August (low season)	For southern parts of the state there are three important words: *hot! hot! hot!* Bring lots of sunscreen, a big hat, and plan on investing in multiple bottles of cold spring water. This is, however, the most affordable time of the year.
	September to November (shoulder season)	You'll undoubtedly discover less competition for hotels rooms and restaurant reservations. The weather will be mild and comfortable. At some smaller airports there may be limited flight schedules.
New Mexico	June to August; December to March (high season)	The summer months are, quite often, the most popular time to visit (with the exception of the excellent winter skiing in northern New Mexico). The weather in the southern regions is excellent; however, lodging prices may be a little higher this time of year (it's those eastern "snowbirds," don't you know).
	April to May; September to November (shoulder season)	Temperatures will be slightly cooler and more hotel rooms will be available at reasonable prices. Some shops may be closed during this slack time.

WHAT TO BRING

Duplicate this section and place it inside your suitcase. Use it as a checklist to be sure you bring the stuff you'll need to make your Southwestern adventure memorable as well as comfortable. (You really don't want to alarm the neighbors about how you were rushed to the hospital in Tucson because you didn't slather yourself with enough sunscreen and eventually wound up with a third-degree sunburn.)

- ❏ **Sunscreen** (a minimum of SPF-50)—lots of it!
- ❏ **Sunglasses** (polarized are best)
- ❏ **A wide-brimmed hat** (a good excuse to purchase that 10-gallon cowboy hat you've always wanted).
- ❏ **Binoculars** (a must-have in these wide open spaces)
- ❏ **Comfortable walking shoes** (3-inch heels are strongly discouraged)

- ❏ **Layers of clothing** (many first-time visitors are surprised to learn that it does get cold in the desert—particularly when the sun goes down and you're out in the middle of nowhere). You'll thank me later for suggesting you toss a sweater or sweatshirt into your suitcase.

- ❏ **A complete set of up-to-date road maps** (your friends at AAA have some of the best). Tip: Don't over-rely on the GPS system in your car. They are not always as accurate (or direct) as you would like them to be—particularly if you decide to go "off the beaten track." Two important tips: (1) Try to stay "on the beaten track," and (2) remember, maps + GPS = good travel planning.

- ❏ **A book, pamphlet, or brochure on desert survival techniques.** Read it before you come and have it with you when you travel. Please don't make your first trip to the desert your last trip!

- ❏ **A spirit of adventure.** Bring an open mind, a sense of humor, and a willingness to try new things and you'll find your dinosaur discoveries trip to be incredibly memorable and delightfully engaging.

Don't forget to bring your spirit of adventure!

NOT TO BE MISSED

It's your first trip to the Southwest—and guess what? You won't be able to see everything. There's just not enough time (not to mention the price of gasoline to travel to every place) to get this whole area into your itinerary.

So, you're going to have to prioritize—what do you really want to see; what do you really want to experience? What are your interests and what would you like to take away in the form of photos or stories to share with the neighbors and friends back home? Again, so many choices and so little time!

First, here are two lists—one for Arizona and one for New Mexico—on the sites that are most often visited by tourists to the Southwest. These are the attractions that get the greatest number of visitors year in and year out. You might want to consider adding a few of these sites to your dinosaur journeys across the region, to give you a well-rounded perspective on everything the Southwest has to offer.

Boot Hill Cemetery in Tombstone, AZ

1. Grand Canyon National Park, Grand Canyon If you visit Arizona and don't see this national treasure, then shame on you!

2. Saguaro National Park, Tucson That great icon of the American West—the saguaro cactus—is scattered throughout this impressive park.

3. Tempe Town Lake, Tempe   Everything from boating to volleyball can be found at this urban oasis, which gets nearly 3 million visitors a year.

4. London Bridge, Lake Havasu Remember singing "London Bridge is falling down" when you were a kid? Well, it didn't actually fall down—it was transported (stone by stone) to Arizona.

5. Canyon de Chelly, Chinle This incredible site consists of many well-preserved ancient ruins amid spectacular sheer red cliffs. One of my favorites!

6. South Mountain Park, Phoenix This park in Phoenix is the largest city park in the United States and one of the largest urban parks in the world.

7. Glen Canyon Recreation Area, Page Encompassing over 1.2 million acres, Glen Canyon National Recreation Area offers unparalleled opportunities for water-based and backcountry recreation.

8. Lake Mead Recreation Area, Boulder City, Nevada If you can do it on the water, then you can do it at Lake Mead . . . every water sport imaginable is here.

9. Phoenix Zoo, Phoenix This zoo was recently voted one of the nation's top five zoos for kids.

10. Tombstone As they say on the brochure, "Visit Tombstone, Arizona, and you'll step back into the rough and tough days of western history."

1. International UFO Museum, Roswell

   Did UFOs land here in 1947? Discover the answer (and all things alien) in this unique museum and equally unique town (*Star Trek* costumes are optional).

2. Gila Cliff Dwellings National Monument, Silver City

   Here you can see unique cliff dwellings constructed by Native Americans centuries ago.

3. Chaco Canyon National Historic Park, Nageezi

   From AD 850 to 1250, this land was rich with the culture of the Pueblo Indians. This is a rare opportunity to step back in time.

4. White Sands National Monument, near Alamogordo

   300 square miles of brilliant white dunes sprawl across a vastness that is unparalleled and unequaled.

5. Cumbres and Toltec Scenic Railroad, Chama

   Travel on an old-time railroad that will take you back in history and through some of the most scenic vistas in the state.

6. Palace of the Governors, Santa Fe

   Built in 1610, this unique

UFO Museum.

The Sandia Peak Tramway provides a bird's-eye view of Albuquerque.

piece of history houses an intriguing and amazing collection of art, history, and New Mexican culture.

7. Sandia Peak, Albuquerque
   The Sandia Peak Tramway bills itself as the "world's longest" and the view from the top will literally suck the oxygen from your lungs.

8. Albuquerque International Balloon Festival—Albuquerque
   Each October, at the Albuquerque International Balloon Festival, the skies are filled with a palette of colors as balloonists participate in awesome displays. You can go up, too!

9. Billy the Kid Museum, Fort Sumner
   60,000 relics await visitors to this engaging museum—including the notorious bad guy's very own chaps and rifle.

10. Carlsbad Caverns National Park—Carlsbad
    This park is world famous for its gorgeous underground caverns. No visit to New Mexico would be complete without a journey here.

White Sands National Monument

Palace of the Governors

Cliff dwellings abound throughout the Southwest.

The next two lists are my personal favorites. The items here will provide you with unique experiences that will last a lifetime, fill your camera's memory card with thousands of images, and offer fascinating stories to share around the water cooler at work (or the dining room table at home) for years to come. Combine some of these with the dinosaur destinations presented in chapter 6 and you'll have a Southwestern adventure that will be the envy of all.

ARIZONA

- ▶ Arizona–Sonora Desert Museum
- ▶ Canyon de Chelly
- ▶ Grand Canyon (see note above)
- ▶ Jerome
- ▶ Meteor Crater
- ▶ Monument Valley

- ▶ Navajo National Monument
- ▶ Organ Pipe Cactus National Monument
- ▶ Painted Desert/Petrified Forest
- ▶ Sedona/Oak Creek Canyon
- ▶ Sunset Crater National Monument

NEW MEXICO

- Acoma Pueblo
- Carlsbad Caverns National Park
- El Malpais National Monument
- Four Corners Monument
- Ghost Ranch

- Petroglyph National Monument
- Shiprock
- Taos Pueblo
- Very Large Array
- White Sands National Monument

The only place in the U.S. where the corners of four states meet.

▶ Arizona observes mountain standard time on a year-round basis. The one exception is the Navajo Nation, located in the northeast corner of the state, which observes the daylight savings time change.

▶ The age of a saguaro cactus is determined by its height.

▶ The amount of copper used in the roof of the Capitol Building of Arizona is equivalent to that in 4,800,000 pennies.

▶ The name "Arizona" is a Spanish version of the Pima Indian word *arizonac* for "little spring place." The Aztec version is *arizuma,* meaning "silver-bearing."

▶ Phoenix, the state's capital, was started as a hay camp.

▶ The bola tie is the official state neckwear.

▶ Five different flags (including the Confederate flag) have all flown over the land area that has become Arizona.

▶ The original London Bridge was shipped stone by stone and reconstructed in Lake Havasu City.

▶ Santa Fe is the highest capital city in the United States, at 7,260 feet above sea level.

▶ The Rio Grande is New Mexico's longest river and runs the entire length of the state.

▶ White Sands National Monument is a desert not of sand but gleaming white gypsum crystals.

▶ One-quarter of New Mexico is forested, and the state has seven national forests, including the nation's largest, the 3.3-million-acre Gila National Forest.

▶ The Palace of Governors in Santa Fe is the oldest government building in the United States.

▶ New Mexico has more sheep and cattle than people.

▶ New Mexico was named by 16th-century Spanish explorers who hoped to find gold and wealth equal to Mexico's Aztec treasures.

▶ Native Americans have been living in New Mexico for some 20,000 years.

Gila National Forest, NM

HELPFUL INFORMATION

National and State Parks

Both Arizona and New Mexico have an incredible array of national and state parks—places where the Southwest comes alive and where you can get a true flavor for this distinctive part of the country. Whether you're wandering over the countryside by vehicle, trekking from large town to large town, or just looking for a little Southwestern action, you can't miss with these spectacular places. You'll definitely want to include a few of these sites in your travel plans—places where you can learn and appreciate the ecology, environment, and scenery of this wonderland.

- ▶ Arizona State Parks (www.pr.state.az.us)
- ▶ New Mexico State Parks (www.emnrd.state.nm.us/prd)
- ▶ Arizona's National Parks and Monuments (www.nps.gov/state/az/index.htm)
- ▶ New Mexico's National Parks and Monuments (www.nps.gov/state/nm)

The "grandest" of them all!

Southwestern Tourism

Both New Mexico and Arizona have tourism bureaus that are nothing short of incredible. A raft of services, information, directions, and must-sees are available for both first-time tourists and seasoned travelers. I frequently use these sites when I travel and have found them to be invaluable in planning any venture through the Southwest.

▶ Arizona Office of Tourism (www.arizonaguide.com)

▶ New Mexico Department of Tourism (www.newmexico.org)

▶ Arizona museums and other cultural offerings (www.arizonaguide.com/things-to-do/arts-culture/art-galleries -museums)

▶ New Mexico museums and other cultural offerings (www.nmculture.org)

▶ Arizona Museum of Natural History (http://azmnh.org)

▶ New Mexico Museum of Natural History and Science (www.nmnaturalhistory.org)

Magazines

If you have the time, I heartily recommend subscribing to or reading one or both of the Southwest's best magazines—*New Mexico Magazine* and/ or *Arizona Highways*. The pages are alive with color and the articles will inform you about places to see and things to do. You may want to check out copies from your local public library or access information from each magazine's website.

▶ *New Mexico Magazine* (1-800-898-6639; www.nmmagazine .com/)

▶ *Arizona Highways* (1-800-543-5432; www.arizhwys.com/)

II. PREHISTORIC STUFF

Chapter 3

Southwestern Paleontology (A Very Short Course)

Dinosaurs came in many different sizes, from large to small.

What follows is a very brief (promise!) course in paleontology. There are no papers to write, no quizzes to take, and no final exams to cram for. It's short and sweet and will provide you with some pretty incredible information about the world we live in and what we've learned about the Southwestern dinosaurs that used to inhabit this world.

Now, ask the next ten people you meet to define *paleontology* and most of them will say it's the science that studies dinosaurs. They would . . . sort of . . . be correct. It's true that many paleontologists examine the life and

Although dinosaurs died out about 65 million years ago, they're actually still around today!

death of dinosaurs, but the field itself is much broader than that. A more accurate definition of *paleontology* (at least according to Wikipedia) would be that it is "the study of prehistoric life, including organisms' evolution and interactions with each other and their environments." Many folks understand paleontology as an area of science that incorporates some elements of biology, along with some elements of geology to understand life in the past.

Paleontological observations have been documented as far back as the 5th century BC. However, the science didn't become fully established until the 18th century and then saw

A paleontologist at work

rapid development throughout Europe in the 19th century. Today, paleontology is markedly different than it was even a hundred years ago. Now the field incorporates elements of archaeology, mathematics, chemistry, engineering, ecology, environmental history, anatomy, biology, and physics into a science that is expansive and far reaching. It would be safe to say that there are many subdivisions in the field of paleontology—all geared to better understand life in the past.

It's Moving

The Earth is not static—it is forever in motion: slowly sliding, shifting and moving. Large sections continuously grind their way over and under each other, earthquakes rip through the Earth's crust with daily regularity,[6] volcanoes belch molten lava from subterranean bowels, and

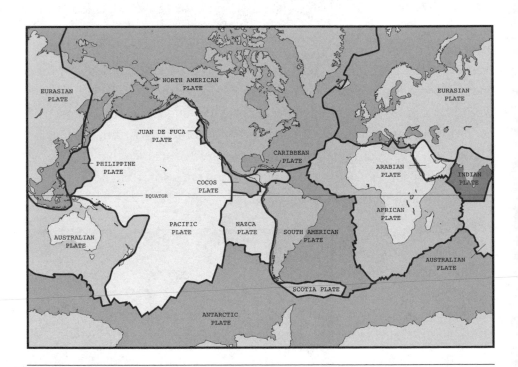

6 The US Geological Survey estimates that several million earthquakes occur in the world each year. Many go undetected because they hit remote areas or have very small magnitudes. The National Earthquake Information Center now locates about 50 earthquakes each day, or about 20,000 a year.

wind and waves sandpaper the fragile surface time and time again. The Earth changes—it is never exactly the same from one day to the next, or from one eon to the next. It is constantly evolving.

We know that the structure of the Earth is dynamic—as it has been for millions of years. The continents are part of large plates—tectonic plates—that slowly move about over the surface of the planet. This concept was first proposed in 1912 by German meteorological pioneer and polar explorer Alfred Wegener, who opined that nearly 225 million years ago there was a single landmass on the planet Earth—a supercontinent. He gave this landmass the name Pangaea (which, in Greek, means "entire earth"). Unfortunately, his ideas were considered far too radical, and for decades both Wegener and his theory were denounced and ridiculed. It wasn't until the 1960s, when numerous discoveries proved the existence of continental drift, that his hypothesis was finally accepted by the scientific community, as it still is today.

Imagine, if you will, several blocks of paraffin (candle wax) on a hot plate. As the undersides of those blocks get warm, they become softer and melt. Eventually the blocks begin to slide around the surface of the hot plate. The same thing is happening to the continents—they, too, slide around on the surface of the Earth. At certain places, molten rock forces its way to the surface to form new plate material. At other places, old plate material melts and is swallowed up in the Earth's mantle.

Basically, our planet is composed of three layers—(a) the crust (the continental crust is about 19 miles thick; the oceanic crust is 4 to 7 miles thick); (b) the mantle (which is about 1,800 miles thick and makes up nearly 80 percent of the Earth's volume); and (c) the core (divided into an inner core about 780 miles thick and an outer core 1,370 miles thick). It is the crust that is synonymous with our paraffin blocks and upon which Wegener founded his original ideas about continental drift.

The fact that these plates are sliding around all the time means that the geography of the world is in constant flux. Right now, for example, America is moving away from Europe, Australia is drifting northward, and Africa continues to separate itself from South America. As further evidence for this continental shifting, consider that the Atlantic Ocean is 30 feet wider now than it was when Columbus crossed it in 1492. It is safe to say that millions of years from now the Earth will look considerably different than it does now.[7]

Then, about 200 to 146 million years ago (and just as Wegener proposed), this supercontinent began to break up. It was like a colossal cosmic fork cutting into a slice of warm cherry pie—separating this wedge of geological dessert into two distinct parts—Laurasia (the northern supercontinent that included the present-day landmasses of North America, Europe, and Asia) and Gondwana (the southern supercontinent that included the present-day landmasses of Antarctica, South America, Africa, Madagascar, Australia, New Zealand, and India).

Over tens of millions of years, the splitting of landmasses continued. Great masses of land broke free of both Laurasia and Gondwana, leaving visual and geological traces of their past relationships (get a map of the world and take a look at the eastern coast of South America and the western coast of Africa—you will easily see how those two continents were once part of a larger landmass.).

As landmasses separated they drifted away from each other—similar to how our paraffin blocks would separate on a warm hot plate. Oceans also widened and expanded, as they are continuing to do today. What was once a single continent (Pangaea) has over considerable time evolved into (today's) seven distinct continents—or, what was once a complete cherry pie has, through continuous rifting and shifting, turned into a collection of considerably smaller cherry tarts (geologically speaking, that is).

---

7 At least one scientist has predicted that 50 million years from now, Africa will have plowed into Europe, Los Angeles will have moved up the West Coast into Alaskan waters, and Antarctica will have moved into the Indian Ocean, shedding its icecap.

It Takes Time

For many folks—particularly those of us well into our fifth or sixth decade—talk of time can be difficult. It becomes especially challenging when we consider time in the context of the Earth's history—4.6 billion years.[8]

Paleontologists traditionally divide those 4.6 billion years into more comprehensible sections known as eras. There are four primary eras in the Earth's history. These include:

The Precambrian era (4,600 to 542 million years ago)—This time frame runs from approximately the time the Earth was formed to the time when some of the first life forms (invertebrates) began to dominate the oceans. Interestingly, the Precambrian accounts for approximately 88 percent of all geologic time.

The Paleozoic era (542 to 251 million years ago)—This time frame, also known as the "Time of Early Life," saw the rise of large reptiles and the first modern plants. It ended with the largest mass extinction in the Earth's history.

The Mesozoic era (251 to 65.5 million years ago)—Also known as the "Age of Dinosaurs" it encompasses three distinct periods of time—the Triassic, the Jurassic, and the Cretaceous (see below). It is also the time when great geological events were dramatically changing the structure and design of the Earth.

The Cenozoic era (65.5 million years ago to the present)—Also known as the "Time of Recent Life," the Cenozoic is when the continents moved into their present positions and the Earth entered into a period of long-term cooling.

---

8 About 15 billion years ago. a tremendous explosion started the expansion of the universe. This is known as the big bang theory. Since the big bang, the universe has been constantly expanding (as it still does today). Some scientists have theorized that the Earth was initially spit out of the Sun as a molten glob about 4.55 billion years ago. Thus, our planet is a relative youngster, when compared to the rest of the universe.

Because this is a very brief course on the science of paleontology, we're going to skip three of those eras (your professor's prerogative) and focus our attention on just one—the "Age of Dinosaurs" (a.k.a. the Mesozoic era), with particular emphasis on the Southwest.

What follows are three charts that will provide you with a quick and easy reference to this prehistoric time. By the way, you're welcome to print these out on index cards and tuck them into your pocket or purse in advance of your next social function or neighborhood block party . . . they'll make great conversation starters!

The Triassic Period

Period	"Triassic" refers to the threefold division of rocks of this age in Germany.
Time Frame	251.0 to 199.6 million years ago
Southwestern Geology	All the continents were part of a single landmass known as Pangaea. For most of the Mesozoic era, western North America was isolated from the rest of the continent by a waterway known as the Great Interior Seaway.
Southwestern Climate	The Triassic climate was generally hot and dry. This seasonally arid climate supported heavily vegetated floodplains. Hot summers and cold winters were the norm.
Representative Southwestern Dinosaurs	▶ *Arizonasaurus* ▶ *Chindesaurus* ▶ *Coelophysis* ▶ *Revueltosaurus* ▶ *Tawa hallae*

The Jurassic Period

Period	"Jurassic" refers to the Jura Mountains, located between France and Switzerland, where rocks of this age were first studied.
Time Frame	199.6 to 145.5 million years ago
Southwestern Geology	In the early part of this era, a great sand sea spread across much of the western interior. Later, a large saline sea extended across the eastern Colorado Plateau.
Southwestern Climate	Arid conditions continued into the Jurassic and giant sauropod dinosaurs roamed the coastal plains.
Representative Southwestern Dinosaurs	▶ Allosaurus ▶ Diplodocus ▶ Ammosaurus ▶ Massospondylus ▶ Apatosaurus ▶ Saurophaganax ▶ Camarasaurus ▶ Scutellosaurus ▶ Dilophosaurus ▶ Seismosaurus ▶ Stegosaurus

The Cretaceous Period

Period	"Cretaceous" refers to extensive deposits of chalk (_creta_ in Latin) along the English Channel between France and England.
Time Frame	145.5 to 65.5 million years ago
Southwestern Geology	Mountain building continued in the western part of Arizona, while shallow seas flooded into northeastern and southeastern parts of the state. The seas also flooded the eastern part of New Mexico, where dense jungles and coal-forming swamps hugged the coastline.
Southwestern Climate	The Cretaceous was a period with a relatively warm climate. This was due in large measure to an increase in volcanic activity, which produced large quantities of carbon dioxide.
Representative Southwestern Dinosaurs	▶ _Acrocanthosaurus_ ▶ _Alamosaurus_ ▶ _Bistahieversor_ ▶ _Daspletosaurus_ ▶ _Kritosaurus_ ▶ _Nodocephalosaurus_ ▶ _Nothronychus_ ▶ _Ojoceratops_ ▶ _Pachycephalosaur_ ▶ _Parasaurolophus_ ▶ _Pentaceratops_ ▶ _Sonorasaurus_ ▶ _Tyrannosaurus rex_ ▶ _Zuniceratops_

Dinosaurs—What Are They?

Dinosaurs are a diverse group of reptiles—by some estimates, representing as many as 1,000 different species. There were large dinosaurs and small ones, two-footed dinosaurs and four-footed ones, carnivorous species and herbivorous ones, as well as slow ones and fast ones (similar to the diversity of modern-day mammals). Dinosaurs were, in fact, the dominant vertebrates for approximately 165 million years of the Earth's history. Equally interesting, they were widespread throughout the world—their fossil remains have been located on every continent, including Antarctica (to date, eight different dinosaur species have been discovered there).

Nope—no human footprints here!

Dinosaurs arose in the late Triassic period and lived (as a group) until the end of the Cretaceous. The fossil record strongly suggests that modern-day birds evolved from theropod (two-footed, lizard-hipped) dinosaurs during the Jurassic period. Most paleontologists regard them as the only group of dinosaurs surviving to the present day.

However, before we continue our dinosaurian journey, we should probably answer that all-encompassing question: What, exactly, is a dinosaur? We'll get to that answer soon, but first let's spend some time with the word *dinosaur* itself.

Professor Richard Owen at London's Royal College of Surgeons was a widely published author who wrote a diverse collection of articles on both living and extinct species. He tended to specialize in shellfish, the nautilus, and certain parasites that feed on humans.

Sir Richard Owen (and friend)

In 1841, Owen came up with the word *dinosauria* for what he called "a distinct tribe or suborder of saurian reptiles." Owen created the name using ancient Greek—*deinos*, which means "terrible," and *saura/sauros*, which means "lizard" or "reptile." Thus, we now have the term *dinosaur* that literally means "terrible lizard" (even though we now know most dinosaurs were placid, noncombative herbivores).

But the question still remains—what is a dinosaur? Dinosaurs were not, as some suggest, supersize versions of most modern reptiles. Most extant species of reptiles have cup-shaped hip sockets. Dinosaurs, on the other hand, had openings in their hip sockets and a unique stance. Most reptiles' legs (such as those of lizards, turtles, and crocodiles) sprawl sideways from their body. In fact, early depictions of dinosaurs (in the late 1800s and early 1900s) mistakenly illustrated creatures whose legs were sprawled out to the sides (as a result of the artists' familiarity with more common reptiles). Yet with their unique hip socket, dinosaurs had legs that extended straight down beneath their body, allowing those legs to support a

Dinosaurs had legs that were relatively straight and positioned directly below the body.

greater body weight. There is considerable speculation that the upright posture and erect gait of dinosaurs was not only efficient and energy saving, but may have been a factor in their longevity.

While most people would state with some degree of certainty that there are two main categories of dinosaurs—carnivores (meat eaters) and herbivores (plant eaters), this is only

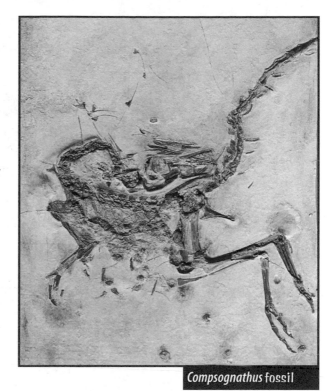

Compsognathus fossil

partially correct. Yes, there are two subgroups of dinosaurs. However, the first is known as the saurischian, or "lizard-hipped," dinosaurs. In these creatures, the pubis bone projected at an angle down and forward. The saurischians include all of the carnivorous dinosaurs from some of the largest (e.g., *Giganotosaurus*, which was 43 feet long and weighed 6 tons [12,000 pounds]) all the way down to some of the smallest (*Compsognathus*, which was 3 feet long and weighed 6 1/2 pounds). A very small number of herbivorous sauropods, such as *Diplodocus* and *Apatosaurus*, are also included in this group. Sauropods are a subgroup of the saurischian dinosaurs. Typically they were four-legged and herbivorous, and had long necks and equally long tails. Many were distinguished by relatively small skulls (and equally small brains).

The second subgroup of dinosaurs is known as ornithischian, or "bird-hipped," dinosaurs. Members of this group have a pubis that is roughly parallel to the ischium ("seat bone"). Both of these bones are directed down and back. The ornithischians are represented only by herbivorous dinosaurs and include *Triceratops, Stegosaurus,* and *Iguanodon.*

Compsognathus fossil

We know that dinosaurs appeared on Earth during the Triassic period and they survived as a group until the end of the Cretaceous, a time span of about 165 million years of the Earth's history. Two of the oldest known dinosaurs were *Eoraptor* (a fast-running predator that also happened to have some herbivore teeth) and *Herrerasaurus* (a bipedal carnivore 10 to 20 feet in length, with curved sharp claws). Both of these early dinosaurs have been discovered in Argentina—in rocks that are 228 million years old. At the other end of the dinosaur timeline is one of the last nonavian dinosaurs on Earth. It was a muscular, swimming duck-billed species—*Arenysaurus ardevoli* (sand dinosaur)—discovered in 2009 in Spain. It apparently lived just a few thousand years before the end of the Cretaceous period.

By comparison, the earliest humanoids appeared about 4 million years ago, and modern humans—*Homo sapiens*—originated in Africa about 200,000 years ago. In short, dinosaurs lived for approximately164,800,000 years longer than humans have been around. Or to put it another way, for every year of human existence, dinosaurs roamed the Earth for 325.

Questions?

It often seems that the topic of dinosaurs generates an extraordinary number of questions—from both young and old alike. What follows are some of the most asked, as well as the appropriate answers for each (in case you want to get ready for the midterm exam):

Did humans and dinosaurs live at the same time? No! Decades of comic strips (*Alley Oop*) and animated cartoons (*The Flintstones*), years of imaginative movies (*Journey to the Center of the Earth*) and library shelves bursting with science fiction novels of every conceivable plot (*Jurassic Park*) have long perpetuated the myth that these two groups of creatures existed simultaneously. Here's the undeniable fact: humans appeared on the Earth only *after* dinosaurs had been extinct for a very, *very* long time (about 65 million years).

Weren't most dinosaurs carnivorous? Typically, when most people (particularly children) focus on dinosaurs, they inevitably think of the largest or most predatory. Nevertheless, the majority of dinosaurs that lived during the Mesozoic era were herbivorous in nature. They often feasted on ferns, cycads, and evergreen trees that covered the land during this time period. At least one estimate indicates that approximately 65 percent of all the dinosaurs that ever lived were herbivorous; the other 35 percent were carnivorous. These figures, of course, do not account for a small group of dinosaurs who were omnivorous (plant plus meat eating).

How long did dinosaurs live? Scientists do not know the exact life span of dinosaurs, but they estimate that dinosaurs may have lived anywhere from the 5 to 10 years of a *Compsognathus* to an almost improbable 300 years for an *Apatosaurus*. Animal life spans relate in part to their body size and in part to their type of metabolism. The maximum possible age of dinosaurs can only be estimated from the maximum life spans of modern reptiles, such as the 66-year life span of the common alligator and the impressive multicentury life span of some tortoises. So many factors affect life span and so much information is missing in the fossil record that the longevity limits of any single dinosaur species may never be known.

Did all dinosaurs live at the same time? Movies, cartoons, and novels would have you believe that all the dinosaurs lived at the same time. Not true. Remember, dinosaurs were around for about 165 million years. Those 165 million years were divided into three time periods

Compsognathus fossil

(Triassic, Jurassic, and Cretaceous) and different dinosaur species lived during each of those periods.[9] For example, an illustration showing *Tyrannosaurus rex* and *Stegosaurus* engaged in mortal combat would be absolutely inaccurate. *Stegosaurus* had been extinct for approximately 80 million years before *T. rex* ever appeared on the Earth.

Epidexipteryx

Were all dinosaurs big? No. Dinosaurs, like the animals of today, came in all shapes and sizes. Some were big, but many were quite small. Here are the current world records (which are always subject to change with new discoveries):

▶ **Tallest dinosaur:** *Sauroposeidon* (60 feet tall)

▶ **Heaviest dinosaur:** *Amphicoelias* (122.4 tons [244,800 pounds])

▶ **Longest dinosaur:** *Amphicoelias* (up to 198 feet long)

▶ **Lightest dinosaur:** *Anchiomas* (3.9 ounces)

▶ **Shortest dinosaur:** *Epidexipteryx* (9.8 inches)

▶ **Smallest living dinosaur descendant:** Hummingbird (as little as a tenth of an ounce)

It would be safe to say that there was a great deal of variation in dinosaur size. It has been speculated that the majority of theropod dinosaurs fell into a range of between 220 and 2200 pounds. This seems to suggest that most dinosaurs ranged in size somewhere between today's female reindeer and saltwater crocodile.

The Demise of the Dinosaurs

There is much speculation and several theories about how and when the dinosaurs finally kicked the paleontological bucket, so to speak.

---

9 The title of the 1993 film *Jurassic Park* (and the book by Michael Crichton) was actually a misnomer. Most of the dinosaurs featured in the movie and book did not exist until the Cretaceous period.

Although massive volcanic eruptions (primarily in India) and changes in climate had already reduced the number of dinosaur species near the end of the Cretaceous period, most evidence seemed to suggest something came from outer space. In 1977, a father-son physicist-geologist team, Luis and Walter Alvarez, were studying some limestone deposits from the time the dinosaurs died out. What they discovered was a fine layer of red clay that contained 600 times the normal level of iridium—an element that is most common in asteroids, meteors, and comets. The clay also contained quartz that had been subjected to enormous pressures that normally happen only when a meteorite hits the Earth. These discoveries suggested that an impact from an incredibly massive celestial object (about the size of the city of Los Angeles) raised a cloud that virtually blotted out the sun and eliminated 99 percent of all living things. The Alvarezes surmised that this object—a meteor—was the cause of dinosaurs' demise.

Later, when other geologists discovered a crater more than 100 miles wide, 12 miles deep, and 65 million years old just off the Yucatán peninsula, the asteroid theory of extinction seemed certain.

Except for one thing. Extinctions rarely happen all at once—they typically take place over time . . . long slices of time. According to the fossil record, we know dinosaurs died out over an extended period of time—hundreds of thousands of years. Thus, it seems likely that the massive volcanoes in India in tandem with the catastrophic aftermath of the Yucatán explosion may have speeded up the extinction of the dinosaurs.

We do know one thing for sure—many other types of life became extinct at the same time as the dinosaurs, including ammonites, many kinds of plankton, and plesiosaurs. On the other hand, many kinds of life *did not* become extinct, including placental mammals (our ancestors), crocodiles, turtles, lizards, snakes, plants, bugs, and the modern-day ancestors of dinosaurs—birds.

After living out their (often short) lives, the dinosaurs died. Their bones and bodies, subjected to the ravages of climate, geology, and time, were transformed into ash, rock, and dust. It has been surmised that 99.9 percent of all the dinosaurs that ever lived have been completely erased from the paleontological record books.

Fortunately, there are remnants of many Southwestern dinosaurs for us to study. Some of these are body fossils (e.g., the skeletons preserved in museums), while others are trace fossils (prehistoric tracks of once lumbering beasts now encased in hardened mudflats). These forms of evidence are the foundation for the next chapter in our discussion of paleontology, and the next chapter in this book.

Chapter 4

Zuniceratops, Dilophosaurus, and Other Southwestern Beasts

When most people think about North American dinosaurs, their minds frequently drift to Montana, Colorado, and Utah. Sure, there have been some impressive discoveries in those states, but they don't diminish the significance of those made in Arizona and New Mexico, which have their own unique panoply of prehistoric beasts—some of which have been found nowhere else on the planet.

T. rex skull

In chapter 3 we talked about how dinosaurs flourished for most of the Mesozoic era—a period of time that lasted approximately 186 million years. You'll also recall that the Mesozoic era has been divided by paleontologists into three separate periods—the Triassic, the Jurassic, and the Cretaceous. Let's take a closer look at those times and at some (but not all) of the Southwestern dinosaurs that were tramping around this part of the world.

TRIASSIC DINOSAURS

The Triassic period began about 250 million years ago and lasted for approximately 42 million years. This was a time when many new species of animals developed. This was also a time when the first dinosaurs were evolving. Evolutionarily speaking, it was very much a time of transition . . . a time of change . . . a time that was a harbinger of the spectacular species that eventually dominated the world of the Jurassic and Cretaceous periods.

Unfortunately, however, the prehistoric record for Southwestern dinosaurs in the Triassic period is remarkably thin. There may be many reasons for this. One theory holds that early dinosaurs were rare and living in places not conductive to the preservation of fossils. Another theory is that significant numbers of dinosaurs may not have migrated or spread northward prior to the end of the Triassic period. Their dispersal may not have been finalized until the Jurassic period—millions of years later.

Nevertheless, a few Southwestern Triassic dinosaurs existed and merit our attention. Let's take a look.

Coelophysis

Although we will study this enigmatic creature in greater detail in chapter 10, I thought I would whet your dinosaurian appetite with a juicy tidbit of paleontological lore. In 1947, Edwin Colbert, a paleontologist with the American Museum of Natural History, excavated

Model of *Coelophysis*

an expansive cache of *Coelophysis* bones at Ghost Ranch, near Abiquiu, New Mexico. It wasn't until 1989, when he published a scientific description of the creature—an article in which he described two adults with the skeletons of young *Coelophysis* in their rib cages—that Colbert pointed out that the juvenile skeletons were too large and too well developed to be unborn babies. As a result, he concluded that *Coelophysis* was a cannibal.

You can only imagine the paleontological firestorm that announcement unleashed.

However, at least one scientist, Robert Gay, has argued that cannibalism has not taken place. Gay contends, "In certain places, both the left and right ribs of the adult overlay the juvenile remains, indicating that the smaller animal is actually underneath the adult." In other words, the larger specimens fell on top of the smaller specimens and were subsequently buried in those positions. He concludes that the positions of the specimens is taphonomic (relating to the decay and fossilization of materials over time), rather than behavioral.

Other paleontologists aren't quite convinced. "It's possible, but I'm skeptical," says Spencer Lucas, curator of paleontology at the New Mexico Museum of Natural History and Science in Albuquerque. "I've always liked Colbert's interpretation that juveniles inside the rib cage of the adults suggested cannibalism." Other scientists weighing in on this controversy mention that cannibalism is a regular and frequent occurrence in the wild. For example, unborn tiger sharks often engage in intrauterine cannibalism—consuming adjacent siblings (in utero) before birth. Upon hatching, large black widow spiderlings often eat their smaller brothers and sisters (typically, less than 25 percent of newborn black widow spiders survive to adulthood). And, for reasons that are not entirely clear, the birth of guppies turns the adults of some species into cannibals. Soon after the the babies are born, the parents will eat their own young. It seems safe to say that cannibalism occurs more often than we would care to admit. In fact, according to some estimates, more than 1,300 species of animals cannibalize their own kind on a regular basis.

The website of the New Mexico Museum of Natural History (http://nmstatefossil.org/item/13) seems to come down unequivocally on the side of cannibalism, pointing out the presence of significant numbers of coprolites (fossil feces), not only in the abdominal cavities of the excavated *Coelophysis* skeletons, but also in the immediate area. Further examination revealed that these coprolites contained small bits and pieces of *Coelophysis*, including teeth, foot bones, and selected vertebrae. Additional evidence suggests that what appears to be "vomit" also contains tiny *Coelophysis* bones. The museum concludes, therefore, that *Coelophysis* was, most definitely, a cannibal.

Suffice it to say that this story may still be evolving as you read this. It is certain that additional data and additional theories will surface in the future. No doubt, this new information will need to be processed by paleontologists before any definitive conclusions are reached.

Tawa Hallae

This seldom seen and little-known dinosaur was initially discovered in 2004 in the Hayden Quarry at Ghost Ranch, New Mexico. In 2006, eight other skeletons (some complete, some partial) were also discovered in this area. This collection of specimens—both adults and juvenile—is probably the most complete assembly of late Triassic dinosaurs known.

The dinosaur's name is a combination of the Puebloan sun god (*Tawa*) and Ruth Hall (*hallae*), who was the founder of the Ghost Ranch Museum of Paleontology. Current estimates place the age of these specimens at somewhere between 213 and 215 million years old— certainly some of the oldest of all known dinosaurs.

One of the most striking, and certainly unexpected findings, was that this dinosaur seemed to be more closely related to several species originating in South America than it was to more familiar (and geographically closer) North American "cousins." This seems to suggest that there may have been a divergence of species in South America (as Pangaea was breaking up), before some of those critters migrated northward into what we now know as the Southwest. Interestingly, it has been suggested that *Tawa's* closest relative may have been the large carnivorous South American *Herreresaurus*—a creature (it has not been firmly established that it was a true dinosaur) from northwestern Argentina and initially discovered in 1958.

The specimens at Ghost Ranch clearly indicate that *Tawa* was a carnivore. Not only did it possess sharp teeth with multiple serrations, it was also had long, sharp claws that were ideal for bringing down a variety of small prey, including fish, amphibians, and reptiles (whose fossils were discovered in the same bone bed). It was also bipedal (two-footed) and may well have been an impressive predator across the ancient Triassic landscape.

The Ghost Ranch specimens are further distinguished by their having had some early avian characteristics (not always expected in Triassic fossils). At least one paleontologist has suggested such features as "proto-plumage" (early featherlike appendages) and hollow air sacs in the neck vertebrae (a characteristic of modern birds). The specimens also revealed open hip sockets—an additional feature of modern-day birds. Suffice it to say, this Triassic dinosaur continues to provide paleontologists with an array of mysteries, conundrums, and puzzles.

The Triassic was not only a time of change. It was also the period when dinosaurs took their place as the primary terrestrial beasts—a role they would not relinquish for almost 165 million years. Although only a limited number of Triassic dinosaurs have been discovered in what is now the American Southwest, that does not diminish their importance or their evolution as the precursors of a reptilian revolution . . . a revolution we are still learning about today.

JURASSIC DINOSAURS

As we have learned, the Jurassic period began about 199 million years ago. During the 60 million years that followed, Pangaea broke apart. The piece of the continent that became North America drifted north, and the piece that became the American Southwest experienced dramatic change. It developed into a great sea of sand, and much of the fossil record of the plants and animals that lived here has disappeared. The evidence that we do have shows that giant sauropod dinosaurs and giant marine reptiles were the predominant species in the Southwest during the Jurassic.

Dilophosaurus

In reality, however, *Dilophosaurus* was somewhat different from the bad-tempered and venomous character that was portrayed as in the movie Jurassic Park, although there are a few similarities. This dinosaur's name comes from the Greek *di* for "two"; *lophos,* "crest"; and *sauros,* "lizard": "two-crested lizard," in reference to the two distinguishing crests on its skull. *Dilophosaurus* stood about 4 1/2 feet tall, was about

Dilophosaurus model

20 feet long, and may have weighed up to half a ton. It was a carnivorous theropod of the Early Jurassic period—inhabiting much of the region now known as Arizona.

Although little known outside paleontological circles (you'll learn more about *Dilophosaurus* in chapter 11), it was the release of *Jurassic Park* in 1993 that ensured its immortality (if not popularity).

Camarasaurus

Camarasaurus was an herbivorous dinosaur of the Late Jurassic period (161.2 to 145.5 million years ago). First discovered in 1877 in Colorado, its bones have also turned up in Wyoming, Utah, and New Mexico. Its name means "chambered lizard"—a reference to the holes in its vertebrae. There is some speculation that these hollowed spaces in the spine saved weight, helping this beast lug its ponderous body over hill and dale. Yet it was not even in the class of oversize dinosaurs such as *Supersaurus* and *Ultrasaurus.*

Camarasaurus

Most paleontologists classify *Camarasaurus* as a medium-size dinosaur weighing in at around 20 tons (40,000 pounds) and reaching a length of about 60 feet. In size it would be comparable to a modern-day humpback whale.

Recently scientists have discovered that some dinosaur bones have growth rings (called lines of arrested growth). For these to be visible, the bones have to be sliced into thin sections and viewed with a polarized lens in the microscope. This process is similar to the science of dendrochronology, in which the age of a tree can be determined by its annual growth rings. It is speculated that the life span of *Camarasaurus*, as was the case for most sauropods, was in the neighborhood of 100 years.

One of the most distinctive features of *Camarasaurus* was its enlarged teeth, each of which measured 7 1/2 inches in length (about the length of an average man's hand). These chisel-shaped teeth were evenly spaced along the entire jaw line and were extremely strong. As a result, *Camarasaurus* was able to eat a wide variety of coarse plant material. However, to sustain its 20 tons of body mass, it would have needed to eat a tremendous amount of vegetable matter each day (by comparison, a 15,000-pound [7.5-ton] African bull elephant needs to consume between 300 and 400 pounds of food every day just to maintain its weight). It's suspected that *Camarasaurus* swallowed leaves whole, stripping them off branches without chewing them. And it would probably have swallowed stones (gastroliths), like a chicken, to help grind food in its stomach. After a time it would regurgitate the stones when they became too smooth. Unusually smooth stones have been found in proximity to several *Camarasaurus* skeletons.

Diplodocus

Diplodocus was a common Southwestern dinosaur during the Late Jurassic period. Its name means "double beam," for certain T-shaped bones in its tail. It was one of the larger dinosaurs of this period, measuring up to 90 feet long. Of that length, 26 feet was its neck and another 45 feet was the tail. It might be safe to say that this creature was all neck and tail and, indeed, it was for a long time one of the largest land creatures ever known. It wasn't until the discoveries of dinosaurs such as *Supersaurus* that *Diplodocus* was "shifted" from the longest to *one of the longest*.

If you think you've seen *Diplodocus* before, you probably have. It is truly one of the most recognized dinosaurs in the world. That's simply

Diplodocus skeleton

because so many *Diplodocus* skeletons have been unearthed over the years, many of which have been placed in a wide range of museums around the world. *Diplodocus* has starred in a raft of dinosaur movies, is a featured figure in dinosaur toys and games, and is one of the most recognized business logos throughout the world.

Despite its mass, *Diplodocus* was more lightly built than other giant sauropods—weighing in at a mere 10 to 20 tons (20,000 to 40,000 pounds). Its forelimbs were slightly shorter than its hind limbs, resulting in a posture that was more or less horizontal. Its elongated neck may have been used to poke into forests to get foliage that was otherwise unavailable to the large, lumbering varieties of sauropods that could not venture into forests because of their size. One recent study, however, suggests that the primary function of the extremely long neck of *Diplodocus* was for sexual display. The feeding benefits of this lengthy appendage were probably only secondary. Fossils of this animal are common throughout the American Southwest with the exception of

the skull, which is often missing from otherwise complete skeletons.

Allosaurus

Until the arrival of *Tyrannosaurus rex* during the Cretaceous period, *Allosaurus* (meaning "different lizard") was unquestionably one of the fiercest and most vicious carnivores of the Late Jurassic period. First discovered in Colorado in

Allosaurus skeleton

1869, specimens of *Allosaurus* have been unearthed throughout the West, including Montana, Wyoming, South Dakota, Utah, New Mexico, and Oklahoma. It is postulated that this creature had an enormous hunting range.

Pound for pound, *Allosaurus* was one of the most powerful carnivores of its time—a virtual hunting machine. In fact, the *Allosaurus* is the most common large predatory dinosaur found throughout this region. It reached a length of 40 feet, stood 15 feet tall, and weighed in at about 2 tons (4,000 pounds). Its rear legs were extremely powerful and exceptionally large. Like *Tyrannosaurus,* it had uncharacteristically short forelimbs ending in smallish hands. However, unlike *T. rex* (who only had two fingers on each hand) the better-endowed (hand-wise) *Allosaurus* had three digits. Each of the fingers tapered into 10-inch, dagger-like claws, which were probably used to capture and hold prey as it was being consumed.

The head of an *Allosaurus* was massive when compared to the rest of its body. Its oversized, powerful jaws contained incredibly large and razor-sharp teeth—teeth that also had sawlike rear edges. By working its upper and lower jaws back and forth to tear its food, an *Allosaurus* was able to turn its teeth into a perfectly coordinated set of dental steak knives. It is suspected that these teeth would have been more than helpful when taking down any large herbivorous sauropods that were abundant throughout the region, and which may have been the *Allosaurus*'s primary prey.

Allosaurus was, arguably, the strongest carnivore of its time. Even though its skull and jaws could bulge outward to grasp huge chunks of meat from any unfortunate victim, there is some disagreement as to whether it was a predator or scavenger (or both). Some scientists speculate that *Allosaurus* may have hunted in packs to bring down larger animals—although there is insufficient data to confirm this hypothesis. Suffice it to say, an Allosaurus herd would have been a formidable and feared crowd on any Jurassic floodplain.

The Jurassic period saw the rise, and eventual domination, of dinosaurs. It was a time of enormous geological and biological change—a time when the world was in flux, when all the magic of evolutionary change was in full bloom. This was true in what was to become the American Southwest as much as it was in all the other corners of the planet.

CRETACEOUS DINOSAURS

The Cretaceous period is often referred to as the last portion of the Age of Dinosaurs, but it was also a time when many new dinosaurs appeared. For example, the first ceratopsian (horned) and pachycephalosaurid (bone-headed) dinosaurs appeared during the Cretaceous. The roughly 79 million years that comprised this period were some of the most dramatic in the overall evolutionary history of the Earth.

Let's examine some of the Southwestern dinosaurs that rose to prominence during this time.

Tyrannosaurus rex

It would hardly seem fair to devote an entire book to dinosaurs of the Southwest without at least a little bit of attention to the king of dinosaurs—*Tyrannosaurus rex*. The pictures, images, photos, and movies in which *T. rex* has been portrayed are simply too numerous to mention. It is, for many, the iconic dinosaur—the sine qua non of prehistoric beasts, and the epitome of fierce, mean-tempered, and generally nasty critters.

T. rex was one of the larger land predators in the Age of Dinosaurs. While not the biggest, it was certainly one of the most impressive. It measured up to 42 feet in length, 13 feet tall at the hips, and up to 7.5 tons (15,000 pounds) in weight. It had a massive skull balanced by a long, heavy tail containing over 40 vertebrae. Many of the bones in the skeleton were hollow—reducing its weight without a significant loss of strength.

T. rex—the most popular meat eater ever!

The skull was extremely wide at the back with a narrow snout—which allowed for excellent binocular vision. It had an extremely powerful mouth that could rip out a massive chunk of flesh with a single bite. Perhaps most impressive were the teeth—in reality, a revolving series of serrated knives. A *T. rex* normally had 58 very large and very sharp teeth that were continually shed and regrown during its lifetime (much in the same manner as modern-day sharks). Each of the teeth ranged in length from 7 1/2 to 12 inches. Suffice it to say, you'd probably want to think twice about facing off with a *T. rex*.

Here are some tidbits of information we currently know about *T. rex*:

▶ Since 1900, when the first T. rex was discovered, only seven skeletons more than 50 percent complete have ever been unearthed.

▶ A *T. rex* brain was about the size of a sweet potato.

▶ *T. rex* may have had infectious saliva used to kill its prey.

- A *T. rex* was about the length of two and a half pickup trucks, slightly taller than a one-story building, and weighed as much as 11.6 thoroughbred race horses.

- *T. rex* had only two functional digits on each hand—most carnivorous dinosaurs had three.

- A *T. rex* foot, with its three digits, is quite similar to a bird's foot, lending further credibility to the belief that birds are "living dinosaurs."

- Scientists have discovered that a large portion of a *T. rex* brain was devoted to detecting and processing smells (for example, the smell of excessive perspiration).

- Although there is no consensus, it is believed that *T. rex* was able to run at a speed of between 11 and 45 mph—with a maximum of 25 mph the most likely.

- *T. rex* existed for nearly 2 million years—which is about 20 times longer than modern humans have lived on the Earth.

Zuniceratops

Admittedly, the word *runt* is not something most people would associate with dinosaurs. To many, dinosaurs are big lumbering creatures that plodded across the Cretaceous landscape with all the grace of an inebriated elephant.

Zuniceratops

And yet a dinosaur discovered in the Moreno Hill Formation in west-central New Mexico could fairly be considered a runt. This critter is distinguished not by its diminutive size, but more appropriately by its lack of dimensions. Known as *Zuniceratops* (Zuni-horned face) this ceratopsian dinosaur was about 10 to 11 feet long and approximately 3 feet tall at the hips. It most likely weighed in the neighborhood of 200 to 250 pounds. Its size would have been comparable to that of a modern-day Shetland pony.

And just to prove that anybody can be a paleontologist, it should be noted that *Zuniceratops* was discovered in 1996 by eight-year-old Christopher James Wolfe, son of paleontologist Douglas G. Wolfe. Christopher's discovery (one skull and the bones from several individuals) was noteworthy for more than just his age. Subsequent dating of the fossil showed that *Zuniceratops* lived 10 million years before the bigger ceratopsians (such as *Triceratops*) of the late Cretaceous period. As a result, *Zuniceratops* is considered one of the earliest-known ceratopsians in North America.

Ceratopsians are a unique group of dinosaurs. Indeed, some paleontologists define them quite broadly as herbivorous, four-legged, elephant-like creatures whose enormous heads sported elaborate horns and frills. Some have even gone so far as to designate these dinosaurs as the most "All-American" of all the dinosaurs, as they lived almost exclusively in North America.

But *Zuniceratops* is a mystery simply because we aren't sure why these dinosaurs would have such elaborate head displays. Paleontologists seem to be divided into several camps on this issue. One group states that the head displays were used to attract members of the opposite sex, while another group is just as adamant that these adornments were used to fend off any predators looking for an easy meal. Others contend that the spikes and horns and frills were used by males to intimidate other males for mating rights. And yet others say that the displays would make a small ceratopsian look considerably larger in the eyes of both predators and prey. And, of course, there are those who suggest that the real reason for these facial features is a combination of two or more of the reasons stated above.

Pentaceratops

Let's take a look at another Southwestern ceratopsian—one just a little bit larger, a little bit bigger, and a little bit stranger. *Pentaceratops* lived during the Late Cretaceous period (99.6 to 65.5 million years ago). Fossils have been discovered in the Kirkland Formation in the San Juan Basin in New Mexico. These critters reached a weight of 6 to 7 tons (12,000 to 14,000 pounds), a length of 26 to 29 feet, and a height of about 9 1/2 to 10 feet. This would have been similar to the more familiar (and certainly more popular) *Triceratops*—a creature who never lived in, or much less visited, the Southwest.

Quite obviously, the *Pentaceratops*'s most distinctive feature was its skull, which is the largest known skull for a land vertebrate and which was almost a third of the length of the entire animal (approximately 7 feet). One skull specimen measures almost 10 feet, the biggest known for any land-dweller. By comparison, our skull is about one-eighth of our height (thus a 6-foot adult human would have, on average, a skull that was 9 inches from top to bottom). *Pentaceratops* means "five-horned face," in reference to the two long spikes that protrude out sideways from under its eyes (these protuberances were technically outgrowths of the dinosaur's cheekbones, rather than genuine horns) as well as the three obvious horns on its head.

To the rear of the *Pentaceratops* skull was an impressive bony frill that often extended to nearly 7 feet in length. There is much disagreement and lots of theories among paleontologists about its function. Some think the neck frill, along with the horns, were used for visual identification and display purposes. In life, the frill's scaly skin covering may have been brightly colored and patterned. The dinosaur may have swung and tilted its head to show off the huge frill area and intimidating horns to greatest effect.

Another camp of scientists believes that the frill helped protect the dinosaur's vulnerable neck area against any would-be predators. Still other scientists postulate that the frill helped this enormous beast regulate its body temperature. And yet one more contingent of scientists believe that it may have been used in mating displays or in helping the *Pentaceratops* identify members of its own species.

There has also been some disagreement among paleontologists as to the function of the horns. Early speculation was that the horns were used for defensive purposes against any would-be attackers. However, current theories postulate that the horns were most likely used in courtship and dominance displays—similar, in many respects, to the way in which reindeer and other ungulates use their antlers.

In spite of its fearsome appearance, this Cretaceous "tank" was an herbivore. It browsed primarily on a range of low-growing plants, which may have included ferns, cycads, conifers, and grasses. Its jaws ended in a sharp ceratopsian beak that it used to bite off the leaves and needles. Given its enormous size, it is likely that the *Pentaceratops* required great quantities of plant material each day to maintain its bulk.

Nothronychus

At least one scientist has said that this Southwestern dinosaur "walked like Godzilla with this big gut." Many folks would probably agree that *Nothronychus* was something assembled by a committee—that is, nobody could agree on what features would make this critter memorable, so they threw everything into the "physiological mix," so to speak. For example, consider the following features:

▶ It was believed to have had feathers, but they were not used for flight.

▶ It had three enormous claws on each front foot.

▶ It had four toes on each rear foot—with all four toes facing forward.

▶ It had a toothless "beak" with dull teeth.

▶ It had a potbellied gut.

▶ It had a tiny head and a long neck.

The name *Nothronychus* means "slothful claw" in Greek. It is a member of a group of dinosaurs known as *Therizinosauria*—a reference to these creatures' most striking features, the three enormous claws on each front foot. There are 28 known species of therizinosaurs, which have been discovered in late Cretaceous deposits in Mongolia, China, and North America. Therizinosaurs were all herbivorous theropods with toothless beaks, birdlike hips, and four-toed feet.

Nothronychus was first discovered in 2001 near New Mexico's border with Arizona in an area known as the Zuni Basin. It was recovered from rocks dated to be approximately 91 million years old. (Another specimen, originally discovered in 1999, was unearthed in the Tropic Shale formation of southern Utah and was determined to be about 1.5 million years older than the New Mexican specimen.)

One of the biggest surprises was the location of the fossil, about 60 miles from the Cretaceous shoreline! The discovery of its large, isolated toe bone came as a surprise to scientists, as it clearly indicated that this was a land-dwelling dinosaur, rather than a marine organism (such as

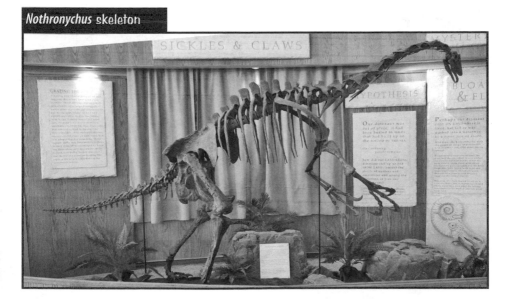

Nothronychus skeleton

a plesiosaur). Thus, the paleontological question became, "How did a terrestrial dinosaur wind up in deposits that were 60 miles out to sea?" (We'll answer that query in chapter 11.)

Excavations by Museum of Northern Arizona paleontologists revealed the *Nothronychus* to be one of the earliest examples of therizinosaurs in North America. Those discoveries showed that *Nothronychus* was bipedal (two-footed) and walked more upright than did many of its ancestors. It weighed about 1 ton (2,000 pounds), was approximately 15 to 20 feet in length, and stood about 10 to 12 feet tall (imagine, if you will, a Komodo dragon with an upright posture).

Reconstructions of this creature's skeleton (from two different species—*N. mckinleyi* and *N. graffami*), on display at the Museum of Northern Arizona in Flagstaff and the Arizona Museum of Natural History in Mesa, portray these dinosaurs as having leaf-shaped teeth with circular roots, a long neck, long arms with dexterous hands and 4-inch curved claws on their fingers, a large "potbellied" abdomen, stout hind legs, and a relatively short tail. In other words—a dinosaur designed by a committee!

Alamosaurus

You might expect that this particular dinosaur's name would mean "lizard at the Alamo"—a creature that was there with Davy Crockett, Jim Bowie, and William Travis in their defense of the historic mission outside San Antonio in 1836. Unfortunately, that would be an incorrect assumption. Instead, the name *Alamosaurus* comes from Ojo Alamo,

Alamosaurus

the former name for the geologic formation in San Juan County, New Mexico, in which it was found and that was, in turn, named after the nearby Ojo Alamo trading post. The term *alamo* itself is a Spanish word meaning "poplar" and is used for the local subspecies of cottonwood tree. Thus, *Alamosaurus*—defined literally—would mean "lizard of the poplar tree."

Fossils of this creature have been discovered not only in New Mexico, but also in Utah and Texas. It was relatively large, measuring up to 69 feet in length (by comparison, the Staten Island Ferry, certainly not prehistoric, is 69 feet wide). *Alamosaurus* also weighed in at around 35 tons (70,000 pounds, or the weight of a four-axle cement truck fully loaded). It also possessed a long neck and an equally long tail (similar to other sauropods such as *Apatosaurus*). There is speculation, at least by some paleontologists, that *Alamosaurus* may have been one of the last dinosaurs to go extinct.

Alamosaurus fossils indicate that it possessed small, almost flattened teeth. These may have been used to strip the vegetation off tree branches or bushes. Several skeletons have also revealed the presence of gastroliths (polished stones in the gizzard), which would have been helpful in digesting the fibrous plants that were part of its diet.

Although they never fought at the Alamo, these creatures may have been some of the last dinosaurs to roam the Earth. Although we still have much to learn about them, they remain one of the "symbols" of this pivotal period of paleontology.

Coelophysis

Sonorasaurus

The Cretaceous period ended cataclysmically, with the impact of a gargantuan meteor. This event marked the end of the Mesozoic era (and the beginning of the modern-day Cenozoic era).

Suffice it to say, the world was forever changed! Millions of years of dinosaur history and evolution were wiped out and furry creatures (a.k.a. mammals) began to dominate the world. Dinosaurs were gone from the Southwest, but they would not be forgotten.

Chapter 5

Dinosaurs by State

Many people are surprised to learn about the incredible variety of dinosaurs that lived in what is now the southwestern United States. Although much of this area was submerged under a succession of prehistoric seas, there were many places where dinosaurs roamed. They may not have been as numerous as those since discovered in Utah, Colorado, and Montana, but they are no less important.

Following are most of the dinosaur genera discovered in both Arizona and New Mexico. It should be noted that some of these creatures have also been located in other states and other countries. No doubt other species of dinosaurs remain to be discovered in both New Mexico and Arizona.

ARIZONA

Fossil remains of the dinosaurs whose names are followed by an asterisk (*) are on display at the Arizona Museum of Natural History in Mesa.

Triassic

Chindesaurus One of the earliest known dinosaurs, this creature reached a length of about 8 feet. It was first discovered in 1985.

Coelophysis* This was a small, carnivorous dinosaur. It has been discovered primarily in New Mexico with a few specimens from Arizona.

Jurassic

Ammosaurus Reaching a length of about 13 feet, this dinosaur was both bipedal and quadrupedal—able to walk on either two or four feet.

Apatosaurus* Also known as Brontosaurus, this dinosaur was one of the largest that ever lived. It reached a length of 75 feet and a weight of around 25 tons.

Dilophosaurus Made famous in the film *Jurassic Park* (the spitting dinosaurs), this "two-crested" dinosaur weighed about half a ton (1,000 pounds) and attained a length of 20 feet.

Massospondylus Fossils have also been discovered in South Africa, Zimbabwe, and Lesotho. First described in 1854, it is one of the earliest-known dinosaurs.

Scutellosaurus Its name means "little shielded dinosaur." Only 4 feet long, it had hundreds of scutes (bony external plates or scales) running along its back and down its tail.

Cretaceous

Nothronychus* A toothless beak, four-toed feet, and birdlike hips distinguished this dinosaur. It also had a potbelly, a short tail, and feathers.

Pentaceratops* A dinosaur distinguished by the five horns protruding from its face (the literal meaning of its name).

Sonorasaurus Fifty feet long and 27 feet high, this is the only dinosaur to have been discovered in southern Arizona. It lived about 112 to 93 million years ago.

Zuniceratops* This is the first North American ceratopsian (horned, frilled dinosaurs), the first with double-rooted teeth, and the first with brow horns.

Zuni Coelurosaur* This dinosaur is a new species not yet named in Latin (its nickname is "Little Tooth"). It was like a coyote, a fast-moving predator that hunted small prey.

NEW MEXICO

Fossil remains of the following asterisked dinosaur species are on display at the New Mexico Museum of Natural History and Science in Albuquerque.

Triassic

Coelophysis* These early dinosaurs had bodies with long legs, a long tail, and a long neck. They weighed up to 100 pounds each.

Eucoelophysis Its name means "true hollow form." This dinosaur has only been discovered in New Mexico and may represent one of the most primitive ornithischians (dinosaurs with a backward-pointing pubis).

Revueltosaurus Discovered by William Parker (who you will meet in chapter 13), its teeth make it look like an early herbivore; although some think it might not be a dinosaur.

Tawa Hallae This 6-foot-long creature might be a link between the primitive dinosaurs of South America and more evolved carnivores of North America.

Tawa hallae

Jurassic

Allosaurus Its name means "different lizard" and its remains have also been discovered in Portugal and Tanzania. This was a predatory carnivore without equal.

Apatosaurus This plant eater had a long neck; a long, whiplike tail; and four massive, columnlike legs.

Camarasaurus The first *Camarasaurus* was discovered in 1877. It has since become one of the most common and well preserved of all dinosaurs. Its name means "chambered lizard."

Diplodocus This dinosaur is the longest (115 feet) known from a complete skeleton. Its neck was 20 feet long, ending in a very small skull.

Diplodocus skeleton

Saurophaganax This dinosaur was the largest carnivore in Jurassic North America. It reached a length of 36 feet.

Seismosaurus This enormous creature (18 feet tall, 60,000 pounds) had front legs that were shorter than its back legs, and also had elephant-like five-toed feet.

Stegosaurus Its name means "roof lizard" and it was distinguished by a series of bony plates along its back. Although the size of a school bus, this dinosaur was an herbivore.

Cretaceous

Alamosaurus Alamosaurus was a long-necked, whip-tailed dinosaur. It was about 69 feet long and weighed approximately 33 tons.

Bistahieversor* This dinosaur had 64 teeth and an opening above the eye that may have accommodated an air sac to lighten the skull's weight.

Daspletosaurus* Related to *T. rex,* it was a predator with dozens of large, sharp teeth. Several scientists place this fearsome carnivore at the top of the Cretaceous food chain.

Kritosaurus* This "separated lizard" (referring to the arrangement of the cheek bones) was a duckbill dinosaur that lived about 73 million years ago.

Daspletosaurus skeleton

Nodocephalosaurus* Little is known about this "knob-headed lizard." Its name comes from a series of oddly shaped cranial ornamentations.

Ojoceratops This dinosaur looks remarkably similar to the more familiar *Triceratops*. It lived approximately 70 million years ago.

Pachycephalosaur* This "thick-headed lizard" looks like a Halloween joke gone terribly wrong. "A face only a mother could love" might be a better name for this creature.

Parasaurolophus model

Parasaurolophus* This critter, too, has some remarkable head adornments. An elaborate cranial crest most likely created a series of sounds used in various forms of communication.

Pentaceratops* This was a rhinoceros-like dinosaur with five horns on its face along with a large bony plate projecting from the back of its skull.

Tyrannosaurus rex* Note to dentist: *T. rex* had a wraparound overbite; when it closed its mouth, the upper parts of the lower jaw's teeth fit inside the upper teeth.

Zuniceratops This herbivore was very small, weighing only about 200 pounds. It had a short frill and stunted double horns over its eyes.

Chapter 6

Tours, Trips, and Travels

ITINERARIES:

New Mexico

3 days

661 miles (approx.)

Grab your cowboy hat, slap on some spurs, and saddle up the rental car for a ride through one of the rootin,' tootin'ist regions of the country. Our 47th state will entrance you, romance you, and enchant you (that's why it's called the "Land of Enchantment") with spectacular scenery and wide, open spaces found nowhere else in the world. Take this trip and you'll record a thousand new memories to share with your grandchildren and all the neighbors back home.

Start off in **Albuquerque** with a visit to one of the great paleontological museums of the world—the **New Mexico Museum of Natural History and Science**. This is the perfect place to introduce the kids to the wonders and magic of dinosaurs. After leaving the museum, head out of Albuquerque on I-40

Walk beside some dinosaurs (at least their tracks) at Clayton Lake State Park.

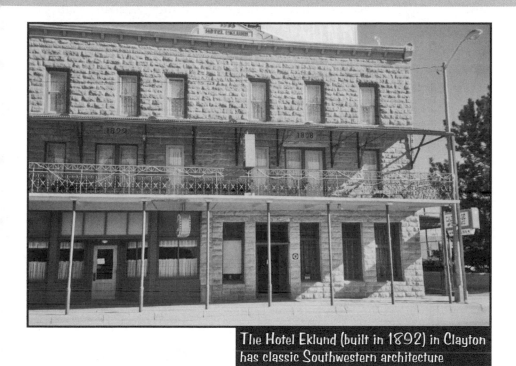

The Hotel Eklund (built in 1892) in Clayton has classic Southwestern architecture

east to the remote town of **Tucumcari** (one of the original towns on the "Mother Road"—Route 66) and the small but fascinating **Mesalands Dinosaur Museum** (the kids will be able to actually touch real dinosaur fossils). Depart town and about 108 miles later you'll find yourself in the tiny town of **Clayton**. Turn onto NM-370 and 12 miles later you'll be at **Clayton Lake State Park**. Watch the kid's eyes pop out of their head as you walk around one of the most impressive sets of dinosaur footprints they'll ever see. Take lots of photos and really impress your colleagues at work.

The dinosaur tracks outside Clayton, NM, have been around for several million years.

After viewing the track site, go back into Clayton and make the long drive (about 4 1/2 hours) to **Abiquiu** and **Ghost Ranch**. You'll fill your camera's memory with this picturesque and dynamic landscape that painter Georgia O'Keeffe immortalized in her paintings. Don't forget to visit the little museum (the Ruth Hall Museum of Paleontology) and learn all about New Mexico's Official State Dinosaur—*Coelophysis*.

Arizona

3 days

535 miles (approx.)

This is the Wild West, folks, and although you may have 350 horses under the hood of your rental car, you can pretend that you're a real cowboy by exploring some of the most remote, picturesque, and photogenic terrain to be found west of the Pecos as well as west of the Mississippi. This is land that sparkles in multicolored sunrises and dazzles in splendid sunsets that will remain in your memory for years to come. This is unforgettable land and if you recall the films of John Wayne, you'll feel as if he's looking over your shoulder at every stop you make throughout our 48th state.

Begin your trip in **Tucson** and the spectacular **Arizona–Sonora Desert Museum**. If you've never been to the desert before, this incredible one-of-a-kind museum will dazzle you with the most amazing collection of desert flora and fauna—including a small display about *Sonorasaurus,* the only dinosaur discovered in southern Arizona. Then, head on up to **Phoenix** . . . no, make that **Mesa** (a suburb of Phoenix) . . . and the **Arizona Museum of Natural History**. Here, you and the family will get a crash course in the paleontology of the Grand Canyon State. Don't forget to hang around for the periodic flood of water over the interior waterfall—it's a sight not to be missed. Load up on water (and lots of car games for the kids) and travel up the road past Flagstaff to just outside the remote northeastern town of **Tuba City**. Just before town, stop and let one of the Navajo guides escort you through an impressive collection of dinosaur footprints. From here you can head on over to that big hole in the ground (the north rim of the Grand Canyon) or down to **Holbrook** and the **Painted Desert** (with colors you won't believe) and the **Petrified Forest** (with trees you won't believe).

The Petrified Forest will amaze every member of the family.

▲▼▲▼▲

DINOSAUR DESTINATIONS

The Whole Enchilada

6 days

1,245 miles (approx.)

This is the real McCoy—a tour through the Southwest that will open your eyes, amaze your kids, and delight each and every member of the family. You can return home with a new swagger in your walk, a new set of vocabulary words ("howdy," "cowpoke," and "chuckwagon"), and that certain confidence that any real cowboy or cowgirl has when moseying into a new town. You'll be singing ballads and whipping your lasso 'round just like any rodeo pro. You've arrived—you're now an official westerner. On top of it all, you will have seen some of the most incredible prehistoric sites to be found anywhere in the country.

Start your venture in **Tucson** and a truly memorable visit to the **Arizona–Sonora Desert Museum** and their interactive display of *Sonorasaurus* (you might want to read chapter 14 first). Then head up the road a piece to **Mesa** and the **Arizona Museum of Natural History**. The kids can walk right up to some pretty impressive fossils and meet several prehistoric beasts face-to-face. Grab the canteens and roll north toward **Tuba City** and the amazing set of dinosaur footprints just outside of town. Be prepared, however: You may get some less-than-scientific information (please read chapter 12). Turn the car southward and gallop toward **Holbrook** and the always spectacular **Painted Desert** and **Petrified Forest**.

The fields around Abiquiu, NM

Next, it's on to New Mexico and the capital city of **Albuquerque**. Run, don't walk, to the best dinosaur museum in the country (yes, the displays are better than that big, fancy museum place in New York City)—the **New Mexico Museum of Natural History and Science** (plan a whole day there). There, the entire family can walk through time while learning about some prehistoric beasts that used to live in the neighborhood. After departing the museum, it's back in the car and up past Santa Fe to the tiny town of **Abiquiu**. Just past the town is the always spectacular **Ghost Ranch** and the surrounding scenery that will transform your eyesight. Stop in at the little museum to learn about the little *Coelopysis* and its amazing story. Now, it's back on the road (a very long road) for a drive across the state to the distant town of **Clayton**. About 12 miles outside town, you'll definitely want to see the most incredible set of dino prints anywhere in the west (oversize photos of these make great additions to the family room back home). After departing the dino footprints, you're headed in a southerly direction to the town of **Tucumcari** and the delightful **Mesalands Dinosaur Museum**. Okay, pardner, now you can catch your breath, review all your photographs, and recuperate from your multistate epic journey.

DINOSAUR DESTINATIONS

4

Get Your Kicks on Route 66

5 days

716 miles (approx.)

Ah, the "Mother Road"—that paragon of cross-country travel that saw millions of Americas climb into their Chevys ("See the USA in your Chevrolet") and hightail it out of town and across the wide, open spaces that were so much a part of post–WWII life. Route 66 is a classic of American history just as much as it is a classic of transportation. Roadside attractions, funky hotels, and the proliferation of "cheap eats" along the byways and highways of America was what Route 66 was all about. It was also about getting out and seeing something other than ubiquitous tract homes and asthma-inducing congregations of smoking factories. It was about freedom! It was about seeing the real beauty of the land.

If you're looking to combine a little prehistoric journey with a trip through more contemporary history, then you'll want to begin this trip down memory lane in the town of **Tucumcari** in eastern New Mexico. Make your starting point the Route 66 Auto Museum and Malt Shop. Grab a malt, see some vintage autos, and then head on over to **Mesalands**

Cross-section of a petrified tree

Dinosaur Museum to see some critters that passed on long before the "Mother Road" was even a glimmer in the federal government's eye. Cruise west past Santa Rosa (which describes itself as the "Oasis on Route 66 and Jewel of New Mexico") and then on to **Albuquerque.** This part of your journey has some of the most authentic parts still remaining

The Painted Desert—a land of contrasts

on the old route so be sure to take lots of photos. While in New Mexico's capital city, stop in at the **New Mexico Museum of Natural History and Science**, and say hello to "Stan"—the very friendly *T. rex* that will greet you (with its ever-present toothy grin) as soon as you walk in the door.

Get back on the road and head on over to Arizona and the **Petrified Forest** and **Painted Desert** region just outside the town of **Holbrook**. Here, you and all the occupants of your vehicle will get a chance to go back in time—way back in time—to see what the west was like long before the invention of hamburger joints with golden arches and gas stations selling vitamin-enriched drinking water. At this point you may want to zig and zag your way off old Route 66 and head north to the dinosaur tracks just outside of **Tuba City**. Then again, you might want to continue your nostalgic journey (away from all those dinosaurs) and through the college town of Flagstaff and on to the vintage town of Williams. A quick drive or a scenic railroad trip north will bring you to the most awe-inspiring prehistoric wonder of all—the Grand Canyon (sorry, no dinos here). All in all, this journey has something for everyone in the car—from the youngest kid to the oldest old-timer ("In my day we didn't have no cars—we crossed this land by mule and by foot. It was uphill . . . both ways!").

DINOSAUR DESTINATIONS

5

Prehistoric Sites and That Big Hole in the Ground

3 days

343 miles (approx.)

If you're really into prehistoric stuff, then this would be your ideal journey. Not only will you get to walk exactly where some big lumbering beasts used to walk, but you also get to stare into the distant past—a past full of unimaginable meteors, unbelievable geology, incomparable geography, and almost incomprehensible fossils. This is a trip that will widen even the sleepiest of eyes and the most closed of minds. Everyone will be jabbering and punctuating the air with exclamations and unreserved excitement. This is a journey that is pure science—science much more revealing and certainly much more interesting than anything your kids (no matter what their age) will ever encounter in a school textbook. This is prehistory at its finest.

Start your trip in **Williams.** Head north via car or railroad to the **Grand Canyon National Park**. Please don't just zip in and then zip out. This venture needs to be savored—at the very least—for a 24-hour period. Put away the cell phones and enjoy the naturalness of this site and one of the seven natural wonders of the world. The time you spend will last forever. After leaving the **Grand Canyon** head on over to **Tuba City** and one of the most spectacular dinosaur tracksites you'll ever encounter (be sure to take a photo of the kids standing inside a dinosaur footprint—it'll make a great Christmas card!). Slide back down Route 89, around Flagstaff, and head west on I-40. After about 35 miles take exit 233 (Meteor Crater Road) and head south for the incomparable **Meteor Crater**. **Meteor Crater** is the breath-taking result of a collision between a piece of an asteroid traveling at 26,000 miles per hour and planet Earth approximately 50,000 years ago. There weren't any dinosaurs around at the time, but it must have scared the (blank) out of any creatures that were in the area. Afterward, head past **Holbrook** and journey through the **Petrified Forest National Park** where you can gaze at 225-million-year-old fossilized trees. By the time you're done, you will have seen some of the most unbelievable prehistoric events, places, and critters this planet has ever known.

"Are We There Yet?"

Arizona: 1 day

118 miles (approx.)

New Mexico: 1 day

124 miles (approx.)

Okay, you have a bunch of kids and good old Granny in the car. You've promised them some dinosaurs, but they're not up for any long-distance car trips. They're not willing to sit still for 4 1/2 hours to see some frozen dino prints in some dirty old rocks. They're cranky ("Why can't we use our cell phones in the car?"), they're easily bored ("If I see one more cactus I'm going to throw up!"), and they always have to go ("I have to go!"). What do you do?

Here are two quick and easy trips you can weave into other travel plans—one for those traveling in Arizona and one for those touring New Mexico. Kids get to see their favorite dinosaurs and you get to say that you provided your youngsters with a scientific experience they will long

Meteor Crater is a distinctive feature of the Southwestern landscape.

remember. Everybody is happy (well, sort of) and they all get what they want.

The Arizona Museum of Natural History has several interesting occupants.

ARIZONA Start off (early morning is best) in **Tucson**. Head on out to the **Arizona–Sonora Desert Museum** (which, depending on the season, opens at either 7:30 AM or 8:30 AM) and let the kids roam all over this desert wonderland. Be sure they stop and see the *Sonorasaurus* display (near the Earth Sciences Center). Pile them back into the car and head northwest on Highway 10 to **Mesa** (Phoenix area) and the **Arizona Museum of Natural History**. Here they'll be able to get up close (and inside) some familiar dinosaurs and see an incredible indoor waterfall that spills over millions of years of history. This place, too, has something for everyone.

NEW MEXICO Begin your trip at **Mesalands Dinosaur Museum** in **Tucumcari.** This is an easy museum to negotiate, kids aren't overwhelmed with a lot of complex terminology, they get to touch and feel lots of different fossils, and they gain an appreciation for prehistoric times. After their museum lessons, head out of town to the northeastern corner of the state and the town of **Clayton**. Wind your way up to **Clayton Lake State Park**, get everyone out of the car, and walk down the path to the dinosaur footprints display at the spillway of the lake. The kids won't believe how cool it is, and when they return to school, they'll probably be jabbering about all the dinosaurs they saw. It's an adventure they won't soon forget.

7

DINOSAUR DESTINATIONS

"We Don't Have Much Time!"

1 day

0 miles

Say your time is short. You've got a thousand places to drive to and a thousand things to see. Your travel funds are limited—gasoline prices are prohibitive, hotels and meals are way too expensive. You want to experience something prehistoric, but your funds and your time are severely limited. What to do?

If you can see only one thing prehistoric in your journey through the Southwest, then that one thing should be the **New Mexico Museum of Natural History and Science** in **Albuquerque**. Please, take it from me—I have visited the Smithsonian Institution National Museum of Natural History in Washington, D.C., the Carnegie Museum of Natural History in Pittsburgh, PA, as well as the American Museum of Natural History on Central Park West in New York City. I have toured dozens of other prehistoric museums—both large and small—around the country and New Mexico has them all beat six ways to Sunday. Some of those big eastern museums have larger collections of prehistoric beasts, but they do not have the sophisticated displays of the **New Mexico Museum of Natural History and Science.** This museum is a class act! Its staff knows how to present their information—information that is not only scientifically accurate, but intellectually pleasing as well. If you can only visit one dinosaur place, this is the place. Trust me, you will not be disappointed!

PREHISTORIC ETIQUETTE

Just outside the town of Grand Junction, Colorado (about 383 miles NNW of Albuquerque), is a place known as Rigg's Hill. On the hill is the Holt Quarry, the site of a momentous dinosaur discovery. It was here in 1937 that high school teacher Edward Holt unearthed the remains of a *Stegosaurus,* an *Allosaurus,* and a *Brachiosaurus.* Holt wanted to leave "the especially well-preserved, articulated fossils intact hoping that they would become a natural exhibit." Unfortunately, what Mr. Holt did not consider was the tendency of humanoid predators to, piece by piece, remove those specimens for their own personal collections (e.g., as a conversation piece for the living room coffee table)—thus robbing the scientific community of some of the most valuable prehistoric artifacts ever discovered. Although the bones were secretly hidden

Some critters may get upset if you mess with their bones

under a blanket of dirt by some local citizens, souvenir hunter after souvenir hunter plundered the site until every last relic of the past had disappeared from the site.

As you might imagine, once dinosaur fossils have been plundered, stolen, or pilfered they are no longer available for scientific study.[10] So, too, are they unavailable for viewing by the public. While you might think that common sense would prevail when people discover such ancient treasures, that's not always the case. Douglas Erwin, president of the Paleontological Society and curator of the Smithsonian's National Museum of Natural History, has said that "theft of fossils from public lands has long been a problem."

Here are a couple of "rules of the road" as you view fossils and other dinosaur artifacts on your journeys throughout the Southwest:

---

10 In 2009, a paleontologist pleaded guilty to stealing the bones of a turkey-size raptor (the informal name for species in the *Velociraptor* genus of dinosaurs) from federal lands in Montana. The value of the fossils was estimated at between $100,000 and $400,000. That same year, the U.S. Senate passed an omnibus public lands bill that includes penalties for fossil theft from public land.

- ▶ Do not (repeat do not) remove any fossils, or things that look remotely like fossils, from any of the places you visit. You'll not only be committing a crime (never a good thing), but you'll be denying the scientific community some valuable artifacts.

- ▶ If you really, really, *really* need some fossils as mementos of your journey through the Southwest, stop in any number of souvenir shops, curio stores, or gift shops in traditional tourist spots and purchase them. The storeowners will be happy to charge you outrageous prices for faux trinkets, facsimile artifacts, and other doodads of the prehistoric world.

- ▶ Remember you are a visitor. In some cases you will be walking across state or federal land. In other cases you will be on private property. If you visit the dinosaur prints outside of Tuba City, Arizona, you will be a guest of the Navajo and Hopi nations. Please behave as you would while a guest in someone else's home.

- ▶ If you're looking at trace fossils—say, the dinosaur footprints outside of Tuba City, Arizona, or the tracks at Clayton Lake State Park, New Mexico—please don't try to make casts or molds of those prints to hang on the wall of your den back home. If you do, you'll actually be destroying part of the prints, which are part of the scientific record of prehistoric beasts.

Tell the kids that, if they don't behave, they, too, could wind up on the wall.

- ▶ Please instruct your children (as well as any accompanying relatives, such as your "light-fingered" mother-in-law) on the need to leave things as they are. Take away the memories, but leave all the artifacts.

- ▶ Take all the photographs and videos you want. Cram that memory card with reams of photographic memories and fill your video camera with tons of movies (don't forget to put at least one family member in a pith helmet for the traditional "I'm not a real paleontologist, but I played one on our vacation" shot). However, let me repeat once more that all the fossils and other prehistoric stuff recorded in these films should remain in New Mexico and Arizona.

"TERRIBLE LIZARDS" & KIDS (THE TWO AREN'T SYNONYMOUS—THEY'RE JUST FRIENDS)

Dinosaurs and kids go together like . . . like . . . well, like dinosaurs and kids. That most kids have a love affair with creatures prehistoric is a given. Maybe it's because these creatures were large and ferocious and kids would like to be large and ferocious—especially when they've been told to clean up their rooms or take out the garbage.

Whatever the reason (and there are probably a thousand of them), you'll find that a dinosaur discovery trip through the Southwest is an exciting way to keep the kids engaged, enthralled, and energized. You may not be able to eliminate "Are we there yet?" but you will certainly provide the kids with tons of stories to share when they come home—stories that will go far beyond the bland facts and dry information in their science textbooks.

Here are a couple of suggestions you may wish to keep in mind when considering a Southwestern dinosaur discovery trip with kids:

- ▶ Take some time to talk about dinosaurs in general before you leave on a trip. Make sure the kids (whether your children or your grandchildren) are up to speed on some of the more familiar dinosaurs—particularly those they will discover in New Mexico and Arizona. Of course, feel free to use the information in this book.

▶ As you are traveling through the Southwest, plan regular opportunities to talk about what you are seeing and how the "up close and personal" encounters are similar to (or different from) what the kids have learned in school. Please don't rush them to a site or a museum without using the experience as a valuable way to converse with them about the value of the experience.

▶ If appropriate, suggest that each child maintain a journal or diary of the sites and museums visited, and the information learned. Periodically throughout your travels you may want to take some time to discuss those observations with your kids. The journals can provide some wonderful opportunities for family discussions—particularly when there is a long day of driving ahead. (Hint: You should keep a journal, too.)

▶ If appropriate, you may want to start a family blog and invite the kids to record some of their experiences for others to read. A blog gives them a chance to communicate their experiences with friends and family back home and to maintain a record of some of the most unusual or interesting places they have visited. Regular blogs are also a great way for kids to keep their writing skills sharp during vacation times.

▶ Make sure kids know the importance of staying on designated trails and of respecting both public and private property.

▶ When you return home, take some time to debrief the kids on what was seen and what was learned. This is a valuable opportunity for children to make connections between real science and the stuff they may get in school. Please plan to visit your local public library and obtain some relevant books (at your child's reading and interest level) on the dinosaurs they discovered and the places they visited.

NEW MEXICO

Chapter 7

The Day I Met the "Bisti Beast" in Albuquerque

When I went to visit the New Mexico Museum of Natural History and Science in Albuquerque, I was greeted by a pair of Cretaceous-age dinosaurs.

Shortly after entering the museum, I found myself face-to-face with Stan. No, Stan isn't one of the more than 300 blue-vested and always cheerful volunteers who work at the museum, rather, he's one of the most famous *T. rex*es ever. Stan is often introduced as the museum's "powerful, bipedal killing machine"— certainly a title that would raise more than a few eyebrows if imprinted on his business card.

Part of the oversize display for Stan includes signage describing his tooth. Featured is a bronze replica of the best-preserved large tooth in Stan's skull— the second tooth from the front on the right side of the upper jaw (in humans it would be known as a lateral

Please don't steal fossils . . . such as this dinosaur tooth.

The 45,000 Bisti/De-Na-Zin Wilderness is a paleontologist's dream.

incisor). My attention was drawn, as yours would be, to the fine serrations along the edges of the tooth—serrations that, like a finely crafted knife blade, helped Stan rip his way through meat.[11]

Incidentally, in the interest of journalistic integrity, it should be mentioned that Stan is not originally from New Mexico—he's actually an invited guest! He's a previous resident of Harding County, South Dakota—a 2,678-square-mile county tucked into the northwest corner of the "Mount Rushmore State" and boasting a total population of 1,353 (2000 census figures). To be absolutely truthful, Stan (named for the person who discovered him—Stan Sacrison) is a fossil replica of the original Stan currently on exhibit at the Museum at Black Hills Institute in Hill City, South Dakota.[12]

---

11 It is also noted that the bite force of a T. rex mouth was something like 1,440 to 3,011 pounds per square inch—which, if you're interested, is the greatest force measured for any animal (dead or alive). By comparison, we humans only exert a maximum of 175 pounds of force with each bite. Just something to keep in mind the next time you visit your local steakhouse (or other carnivorous establishment).

12 For those readers looking to decorate an empty corner of the living room or add a conversation piece to the basement den, you can obtain your own 40-foot replica of Stan directly from the Black Hills Institute of Geological Research, Inc. (www.bhigr.com/store/product.php?productid=46). The price: $100,000 (crate and packing fees are extra).

Although *T. rex* once roamed the Creataceous landscape in what is now New Mexico, there has been a dearth of *T. rex* fossils located within state borders. One of the few discovered—a lower jaw—was found near Elephant Butte Reservoir. In 1983, members of a Las Cruces sailing club stopped on the eastern shore of the reservoir and discovered a tooth. The jaw was collected and became one of the first fossils donated to the museum. Rising water levels prevented the collection of all the fossil material until 2002, when at the height of a drought, museum paleontologists collected the remaining skull fragments.

Next to Stan I see an old friend, *Coelophysis* (actually it's a bronze replica), a creature you met briefly in chapter 4 and one you'll meet again, in somewhat more detail, in chapter 10.

I begin my day's journey on the second floor of the museum—in the section entitled Origins. Here I am presented with interactive displays, engaging exhibits, and fascinating information regarding the beginnings

Hi, my name is Stan!

Elephant Butte Lake

of the Earth and the beginnings of life on this planet (the Precambrian and Paleozoic eras), 12 billion to 251 million years ago.

The next section of the museum—Dawn of the Dinosaurs—presents life in the Triassic era. This was when the world was dominated by a single supercontinent—Pangaea. This period was preceded by the largest mass extinction in the Earth's history. In fact, paleontologists estimate that up to 90 percent of all marine species were eliminated at the time of the extinction.

It is here that I am introduced to an assembly of prehistoric creatures—critters that might well be called the creatures that time forgot. Many people mistakenly believe dinosaurs were the first land animals, or the first reptiles, to inhabit the Earth. In reality, the late Triassic was a world of phytosaurs—a group of semiaquatic predatory reptiles with long snouts and heavy armor. Although they resemble modern-day crocodiles and alligators, they are not related at all. Their remains have been found in North America, South America, Europe, North Africa, Madagascar, and India—a fossil record that adds further credibility to the single landmass (Pangaea) theory.

One of the most interesting displays in this section is entitled "Living Fossils." Here, museumgoers can meet Kirby—the museum's own 2-foot-long lungfish. Lungfish are freshwater creatures that retained many primitive (and prehistoric) features such as the ability to breathe air and the presence of lobed fins. When I observe Kirby in his one-fish aquarium, he reminds me of how I feel without my initial cup of morning coffee—quite listless and not entirely ready for the workday.

Realistic displays make the NMMNHS one of the world's greatest dinosaur museums.

I'm also introduced to other Triassic animals found in New Mexico. These include *Elcyclotosaurus* and *Erythrosuchian*—large predatory reptiles found in the Moenkopi Formation in New Mexico. I also meet several metoposaurs—the last of the large amphibians.

Departing the Triassic period, I am introduced to a most fascinating creature. He's not prehistoric (although he does have a shock of gray hair), certainly not a fossil (although there's a facial wrinkle or two), and arrives without any descriptive signage (although he does sport an official museum ID badge): Just inside the cavernous Jurassic Hall I meet Frank Faustine, one of the museum's amiable, knowledgeable, and gracious volunteers. I learn later than there are more than 300 volunteers

Seismosaurus and *Saurophaganax* even exceed the size of this photograph.

working at the museum—helping visitors understand the various displays, adding a bit of color in their bright blue vests, and helping folks locate various sections of this all-encompassing building.

Frank introduces me to two of the most imposing residents in this section of the museum—*Seismosaurus* and *Saurophaganax*.[13] Having been a museum volunteer for 10 years, Frank has a wealth of knowledge about all the displays, along with a passion for sharing them with the viewing public. A wry sense of humor and an intense desire to "get it right" make our conversation both pleasing and informative. Frank provides me with some insights on the various displays, the bones and

13 Saurophaganax ("king of the reptile-eaters") was the largest meat-eating dinosaur of the Jurassic. Forty feet long and an estimated 5 tons, Saurophaganax was a ferocious ambush predator, like modern-day crocodiles. It killed by slashing the neck of its prey.

articulated skeletons, and the history of these two beasts. He is, as are all the volunteers I encounter during the day, very helpful, very genuine, and very engaging. It is obvious that this is a very proactive museum and Frank is certainly emblematic of the ways in which the museum reaches out to share information with the general public.

Seismosaurus

According to the museum's dynamic and engaging display, the story surrounding the discovery and examination of this gigantic beast is nothing short of amazing. It goes something like this:

In 1979, two hikers were roaming an area northwest of Albuquerque. They noticed several enormous vertebrae weathering out of Jurassic-age mudstones near the top of a mesa. For fear of the fossils being vandalized, they kept their secret—only sharing it with a few close friends. It wasn't until 1985—and increased recreational activity in the area—that the two individuals reported their discovery to Dr. David Gillette, then curator of paleontology at the newly established New Mexico Museum of Natural History (NMMNH).

Over the next decade, several tons of rock and bone were chipped from the site and transported to the NMMNH. Preparators began the arduous process of separating the fossils from the surrounding rock (matrix)—a process complicated by the fact that both fossil and matrix were similar in color, hardness, and in some areas, texture. This process revealed the partial skeleton of a huge new sauropod—one of the longest dinosaurs in the world.

After some of the first bones (vertebrae from the middle of the tail) were prepared, Gillette began comparing them to their counterparts in other sauropods. Although they were closest in form to the well-known *Diplodocus,* they were much larger and differed in their overall proportions. Gillette concluded that they were unique enough to warrant their own genus, and in 1991 he published an article naming the fossil *Seismosaurus,* or "earth-shaking lizard." In his description, Gillette estimated that, when alive, *Seismosaurus* might have been up to 170 feet long.[14]

By the closing years of the 20th century, enough of the fossils had been prepared to begin the creation of an accurate skeletal reconstruction of *Seismosaurus.* As new teams of researchers began to compare *Seismosaurus* to *Diplodocus,* they suspected that some of the bones placed toward the middle of the tail had, in fact, been located much closer to the hips. This realization significantly shortened the animal's overall length; from a near-record 170-foot maximum down to a "mere" 110 feet long (more like our friend the blue whale).

In life, *Seismosaurus* was an enormous, long-necked, whip-tailed, small-headed dinosaur. It was roughly 18 feet tall and may have weighed about 30 tons (the combined weight of four adult male African elephants). *Seismosaurus* had nostrils at the top of its tiny head. Its front legs were shorter than its back legs, and all had elephant-like, five-toed feet. Its short legs may have helped stabilize this enormous dinosaur. One toe on each foot had a thumb claw, probably for protection. Its backbone had extra bones underneath it, which had chevron-shaped bony protrusions running both forward and backward, probably for support and extra mobility of its neck and tail. The tail of a *Seismosaurus* contained at least one unusual wedge-shaped vertebra that gave it a kink. It may have used this whiplike tail for protection.

---

14 For comparison purposes, the blue whale, often deemed the largest animal ever known to have existed, is a mere 108 feet in length (although it does weigh in at a gargantuan 200 tons). A typical 18-wheeler tractor-trailer is about 60 feet in length, with a double trailer extending out to 113 feet. And, just in case you get asked at your next cocktail party, the world record for the longest animal is a bootlace worm washed ashore on a beach in St. Andrews, Scotland, in 1864. The worm was measured at a length of 180 feet. Now, just imagine that critter crawling through the humus in your garden.

Seismosaurus was an herbivore and sported blunt, peglike teeth, useful for stripping foliage. It must have eaten a tremendous amount of plant material each day to sustain itself. It probably swallowed leaves whole, without chewing them, and used gastroliths (stomach stones) to help digest this tough plant material. Its main food was probably conifers, which were the dominant plant when these large sauropods lived. Secondary food sources may have included gingkos, seed ferns, cycads, bennettitaleans, ferns, club mosses, and horsetails. It is speculated that *Seismosaurus* may have travelled in herds and may have migrated when they depleted their local food supply.

In addition to all its physical attributes, the *Seismosaurus* on display also has some international travel under its belt. I learn that it has made two trips to Japan and in 2002 was the star of an exhibition in Tokyo entitled the Greatest Dinosaur Expo.

▲▼▲▼▲

I'm now entering the next large room—another enormous hall that has been ingeniously labeled "New Mexico's Seacoast"—that period of time when an extensive seaway reached from the Gulf of Mexico to the Arctic Ocean—covering most of New Mexico. This is the beginning of the Cretaceous period. Upon entering the hall I'm presented with a "Weather Report for Tropical New Mexico." It seems that the late Cretaceous period in New Mexico was characterized, oddly enough, by tropical conditions. In addition to its warm climate, sea levels were relatively high and there was a significant amount of water vapor and carbon dioxide in the atmosphere. All-around temperatures during this time of the Earth's history were quite high. Cretaceous New Mexico may have been more like modern-day Panama or Venezuela.

One of the first Cretaceous critters I meet is *Pentaceratops*—or, more specifically, the skull of one. As you may recall from our discussion of *Pentaceratops* in chapter 4, this fascinating herbivore, only found in New Mexico, was an imposing figure with its five-horned head.

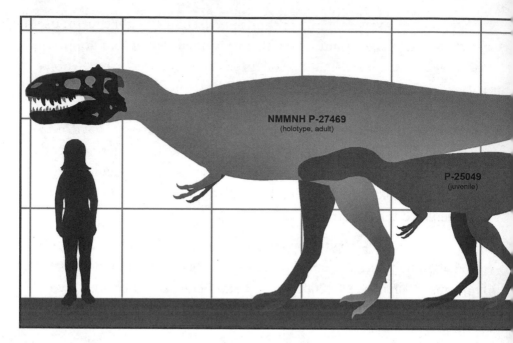

NMMNH P-27469
(holotype, adult)

P-25049
(juvenile)

Some (notably this author) have likened this beast to a rhinoceros with attitude. Suffice it to say, its formidable stature belied its herbivorous diet of ferns, cycads, conifers, and grasses.

One of the questions science has been unable to answer (and one of the questions frequently asked by youngsters) deals with the color of dinosaur skin. In short, what color were the dinosaurs? The answer to that perpetual query is displayed along the walkway that rims the perimeter of this hall. Here I learn that although fossils can preserve the size and habits of prehistoric creatures, they cannot preserve the color of their skin. As a result, scientists often have to guess at each dinosaur's skin color. As several large animals today have drab colors (brown or gray, for example) it's often speculated that dinosaurs (particularly the large ones) may have also been drab. That point is sometimes contested, however, because it has been pointed out that birds, as the only remaining surviving dinosaurs, happen to have good color vision.[15]

---

15 A recent article (www.cbsnews.com/stories/2010/01/28/tech/main6151957. shtml) reported that at least one feathered dinosaur—the *Sinosauropteryx*, which lived in China—had a red Mohawk and a red and white striped tail.

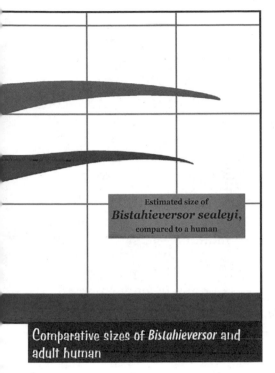

Estimated size of
Bistahieversor sealeyi,
compared to a human

Comparative sizes of *Bistahieversor* and adult human

Walking along the far side of the hall, I come upon another skull in a glass case. This is the skull of a creature—both mysterious and enigmatic—that until 1998 was unknown and undiscovered. It is a creature I had been eager to meet.

It is the skull of the "Bisti Beast."

Bistahieversor sealeyi

Throughout Asia and North America, tyrannosaurs were the dominant predators, particularly during the Late Cretaceous period—that interval of Earth's history marked by high global sea levels and hothouse conditions. While paleontologists aren't certain about the origin of tyrannosaurs, recent discoveries of early primitive (and remarkably small-bodied) Asian tyrannosaurs has provided them with some compelling evidence that the group most likely originated in Asia or Europe during the Jurassic period.

In 1997, a museum volunteer, Paul Sealey, was poking around the Bisti/De-Na-Zin wilderness area near Farmington, New Mexico (a public area managed by the federal Bureau of Land Management). The Bisti/De-Na-Zin area is located in the San Juan Basin—

Two *Pentaceratops*

an area where the rocks are about 73 to 74 million years old. There he discovered surface evidence of a tyrannosaur's skeleton. Sometime later, Dr. Thomas Williamson, the museum's paleontology curator, visited the new site and realized immediately that Sealey had found a very rare and important fossil, the partial skeleton of a tyrannosaur, a member of the group of meat-eating dinosaurs that includes *Tyrannosaurus rex.*

The necessary permits were obtained and excavation of the fossils began in the summer of 1998. The site was located in a rugged, but scenic area. It was far from any roads and all of the necessary supplies and equipment had to be carried to the site by hand. Much of the excavation work was done under harsh conditions—high temperatures, voracious gnats, and physically demanding labor.

By the end of the summer, large blocks of rock containing the dinosaur bones had been safely wrapped in plaster-covered packages and braced with sturdy wooden planks. The New Mexico Army National Guard had volunteered to airlift the specimens out of the wilderness area as part of a training exercise. Enormous helicopters were employed to lift the heavy jackets and fly them to flatbed trailers parked outside of the wilderness boundary. From there, the multimillion-year-old treasure was hauled down to the museum's fossil preparation lab in Albuquerque.

In the lab, the plaster was slowly and methodically removed and the preparators began the long and arduous process of separating the bones from the skeleton. Finally, after two years of painstaking work, the skull was finally released from its stone matrix.

For the first time in 73 million years, the skull of this Cretaceous tyrannosaur was revealed to a most giddy band of paleontological admirers.

The new tyrannosaur was named *Bistahieversor sealeyi* (a name made from combining Greek and Navajo words and meaning "Sealey's destroyer of the Badlands"). It was similar to other tyrannosaurs, including *Albertosaurus* and *Daspletosaurus,* but retained many more primitive features of the skull. These included idiosyncratic features of the snout (it had a deep snouted skull that is characteristic of more advanced tyrannosaurs), a distinctive forehead, and horny projections over each eye. This particular specimen lived about 74 million years ago.

It was the deep-snouted skull that immediately caught the attention of Dr. Williamson and Dr. Thomas Carr of Carthage College. After an exhaustive review of the research they speculated that after tyrannosaurs first dispersed into North America, the rise in global sea level cut off the tyrannosaurs of the East Coast from those of Western North America and Asia. Tyrannosaurs, such as *Bistahieversor,* subsequently evolved deep snouts in western North America and these became dominant there and dispersed back into Asia.

The skull of the museum's *Bistahieversor sealeyi* is ceremoniously displayed in the Cretaceous Hall exhibit. Signage within the display indicates the skull is, in many ways, similar to the more well-known dinosaur *T. rex.* What is even more amazing is that it is an almost complete skull (something not often discovered out in the field)—one of the very few found in New Mexico. Closer inspection reveals several features, several of which parallel those of *T. rex*: very big teeth, a rough snout, and large eye sockets.

An additional specimen representing a subadult about half the size of the adult-type specimen is also on display. This specimen was also collected from the San Juan Basin, from lands of the Navajo Nation. The adult *Bistahieversor* specimen has a skull over 3 feet long; the entire animal was probably about 30 feet long and weighed approximately 3 tons. By comparison, the subadult specimen is approximately half the length of the adult. Studies based on other tyrannosaur specimens show that they attained an adult size in about 30 years. Thus, the subadult was likely a teenager.

Both specimens show scarring of the bone caused by various injuries that were either infected or were healing at the time of death. This is common to many tyrannosaur specimens and indicates that they probably lived violent, and most likely, short lives. It seems that the Cretaceous was similar, in many ways, to life in a classic small town of the Old West. The smaller specimen, for example, has a significant puncture in its lower jaw—something that may have been inflicted by another, potentially hungry, predator. There is also evidence of several facial injuries that may have occurred all at one time or as a result of several encounters with bad-tempered contemporaries. I find it equally fascinating to learn that all of these injuries also indicate a certain degree of infection, which undoubtedly means they happened when the creature was living. No doubt there was some significant pain associated with those infections. It seems that even predacious carnivores with oversized jaws didn't necessarily have it easy.

After my visit to the museum I contacted Dr. Williamson, who graciously agreed to respond to some additional questions I had about this beast. Specifically, I wanted to know why *Bistahieversor* was important—particularly in terms of New Mexico paleontology. Dr. Williamson responded, "Besides representing a new genus and species of tyrannosaur, the presence of *Bistahieversor* in New Mexico shows that tyrannosaurs were very diverse during the late Campanian (approximately 75 million years ago) and show that there was a high level of provinciality among tyrannosaurs (as well as other dinosaurs) during this time in western North America."

It seems that although our friend *T. rex* seems to get all the attention—at least as far as tyrannosaurs are concerned. Apparently, other tyrannosaurs had equally impressive "credentials."

I wanted to know what paleontologists have learned about Cretaceous New Mexico as a result of *Bistahieversor*. Dr. Williamson, both pithy and precise, explained, "The evidence suggests that there was only one tyrannosaur in New Mexico during the late Campanian—*Bistahieversor*. Previously it was thought that the tyrannosaur present in New Mexico was *Albertosaurus*. We now know that *Albertosaurus* was restricted to the northern Rocky Mountain Region (Alberta and northern Montana). Completely different tyrannosaur taxa were living in the Southwest."

As paleontology is an ever-evolving science, I was curious about any new information that has surfaced since the *Bistahieversor* display was set up. Characteristically honest, Dr. Williamson told me, "The most

The northwest corner of Mexico's Yucatan Peninsula, illustrating the Chicxulub impact crater. The top picture is generated by Shuttle Radar Topography Mission (SRTM); the bottom photo, by the Landsat satellite.

significant new thing that we have learned is that the subadult specimen (the panel-mounted tyrannosaur at the eastern end of the hall) also represents *Bistahieversor*. We've known this for several years, but haven't yet changed the signage to reflect our new knowledge. We therefore know a great deal about the ontogeny, or how this animal changed as it matured, for this dinosaur."

The museum, supported by the New Mexico Department of Cultural Affairs, is a public building. Part of its mission is to disseminate information and promote scientific discoveries made within and throughout the state. Thus, I wanted to ask Dr. Williamson why the public should care (or know) about the "Bisti Beast." He kindly responded, "*Bistahieversor* is a tyrannosaur known only from New Mexico. Tyrannosaurs were a group of very large predatory dinosaurs that dominated the Late Cretaceous of the northern hemisphere (an interval of about 35 million years). *Bistahieversor* is one of the most basal, or primitive, members of the tyrannosaurs known from North America. The discovery of *Bistahieversor* has helped us better understand the complex evolutionary history of this group."

▲▼▲▼▲

I continue to follow the walkway down into a section of the museum entitled "A Bad Day in the Cretaceous." A vibrant mural covers the walls, an intermittent strobe light flashes, thunder rolls, and I find myself in an interactive display that recreates the end of the world—or, at least the end of the Cretaceous period. A prominent sign entitled "Extinction Mural" informs visitors about this cataclysmic event. Just like a bad disaster movie (except this really happened), the Chicxulub Impact—that 6-mile long meteor—slammed into the Earth and completely destroyed much of what is now New Mexico, as well as other significant areas of western North America. Not only was there intense heat (causing vegetation to spontaneously combust), but the region was also subjected to gigantic tsunamis and hurricane-force winds. Enormous forest fires raced across the globe and unimaginable amounts of gases and acids were released into the atmosphere. Acid rain fell everywhere. Talk about your bad hair day!

Just after the Earth gets totally annihilated, there's a wonderful display farther along the path called "Dynamic Dinosaur Story." This is an engaging animation about a *Dromaeosaurus* (a small, 6-foot-long carnivorous dinosaur of the late Cretaceous). The display is set inside a darkened, cavelike structure, where a simulated fossil of *Dromaeosaurus* is shown as it might look upon discovery. After pressing a button, the interior of the "cave" darkens, the fossil is outlined in red lights, and then the fossil is magically transformed into an animated figure that "describes" its very brief life as it runs, eats insects, and evades its enemies. However, the animated dinosaur eventually is preyed upon by a larger dinosaur. The animation slowly dissolves and transforms itself back into the fossil. The three minute program is well done—an excellent display for both adults and kids.

Eventually, I wend my way through the Tertiary period ("Age of Volcanoes" and "Evolving Grasslands") and the Pleistocene period ("New Mexico's Ice Age") and around the "Quaking Earth." After another nearly two hours of taking notes and recording impressions, I meet up, once again, with my pal Stan. Although Stan is an unofficial volunteer (he doesn't have the requisite bright blue vest), his presence at the end of my journey is a dynamic punctuation mark for this world-class museum.

NEED TO KNOW

DIRECTIONS From the Albuquerque International Airport head east on Sunport Blvd SE toward Sunport Loop SE. Continue onto Sunport Loop SE and then onto Sunport Blvd SE. Merge onto I-25 via the ramp to I-40 N/Downtown/Santa Fe. After 3.7 miles, take exit 226B to merge onto I-40 W toward Gallup. Travel for 2.5 miles and then take exit 157A for Rio Grande Blvd. Turn left onto Rio Grande Blvd NW and then left again onto Mountain Road NW.

From the airport, the drive is approximately 9 miles.

CONTACT INFORMATION New Mexico Museum of Natural History and Science, 1801 Mountain Rd. NW, Albuquerque, NM 87104 (505-841-2800; www.nmnaturalhistory.org/).

FEES Adults (13–59) $7, seniors (60+) $6, children (3–12) $4.

HOURS 9 AM to 5 PM every day except Thanksgiving, Christmas, and New Year's Day.

Dromaeosaurus skull

BEST TIME TO VISIT Any time of the year. Please be aware that this is a very popular museum, so it will often be crowded (watch for vast and extensive armies of school children ebbing and flowing through the exhibits).

CAMPING/LODGING There are hundreds of hotels, motels, B&Bs, and other forms of lodging—from really, *really* cheap to really, *really* expensive—throughout the greater Albuquerque area. Check out all the offerings at the New Mexico Tourism Department (www.newmexico .org/).

ACCESS The museum is wheelchair accessible throughout.

NOTES I have visited many dinosaur museums across the United States. This one is truly one of the finest. The history of life on this planet is displayed chronologically and accurately, there is a wealth of well-written, informative, and dynamic displays, and the blue-vested volunteers are always friendly and helpful. Take the kids, take grandma, take the neighbors (leave the dog)—it's a day they'll all remember and treasure.

Chapter 8

In Old Tucumcari

Hop on Interstate 40 in Albuquerque and head east for about 175 miles (or 2 hours and 49 minutes of driving time) to the quaint desert town of Tucumcari, New Mexico.[16] Make a left on South First Street and a right on West Laughlin Avenue and you'll find yourself in front of Mesalands Dinosaur Museum—a warehouse-like building (managed by Mesalands Community College) with tan stucco walls and a sky blue roof. But don't let the bland exterior fool you—there's a treasure trove of prehistoric goodies waiting inside—dinosaurs you'll never see anywhere else.

Tucumcari Mountain, just outside Tucumcari, NM

This is the home of bronze dinosaurs—sort of the Hard Rock Café of prehistoric museums.

"Why bronze dinosaurs?" you may ask. Well, the museum has an answer to that eternal and persistent query. Shortly after you enter, you

---

16 Tucumcari (the correct pronunciation is TOO-kum-kair-ee) bills itself as the "Heart of the Mother Road" and the "Gateway City of Murals." Nestled on historic Route 66, Tucumcari is also proud to say it has more than 1,200 motel rooms (I was only able to stay in one of them).

Mesalands Dinosaur Museum is a great place to visit!

come upon a small display entitled "Making Bronze Dinosaurs." It reads as follows:

Why Bronze Dinosaurs?

Why is this museum full of bronze replicas of dinosaurs and other prehistoric animals?

▶ Because they are visually spectacular.

▶ Because you are able to touch them, unlike most genuine fossils and bones.

▶ Because Mesalands Community College has a bronze foundry capable of producing these replicas.

Why don't other museums have so many bronze pieces? Because they are very expensive to produce. The bronze process has many steps and is very labor intensive. To produce the final claw in this case (a 6- to 7-inch-long Allosaurus claw is displayed) took about 40 hours. Imagine doing a complete skeleton with several hundred bones.

The brochure for the museum proudly states, "Mesalands has on display the world's largest collection of bronze skeletons, fossils and replicas of prehistoric creatures. The bronzes were created as part of the college's fine arts program by members of Mesalands staff, assisted by a number of community volunteers."

The first section of the museum presents "The History of Life," featuring fossils of trilobites, ammonites, and stromotolites. There's also a large display of life in the Precambrian, Paleozoic, Mesozoic, and Cenozoic eras—a journey through millions of years of prehistory in the space of approximately 25 feet. This is a dynamic display of fossils from each of the Earth's ages—beginning with microscopic algae and ending with a collection of humanoid and human skulls.

I pass by the display "Dinosaur Droppings" (don't ask) and the museum's paleontology laboratory. Shortly after is a three-dimensional mural, which includes *Gojirasaurus quayi*—the largest carnivorous dinosaur known from the Triassic era of eastern New Mexico or from anywhere else in North America. I also come upon a display of a phytosaur skeleton and a bronze replica of the skull of a *Camarasaurus* (my first "heavy metal" dinosaur).

Positioned on the floor are bronze replicas of two vertebrae of the middle backbone of *Seismosaurus*. As you will recall, *Seismosaurus* was one of the largest dinosaurs to trod this part of the world and

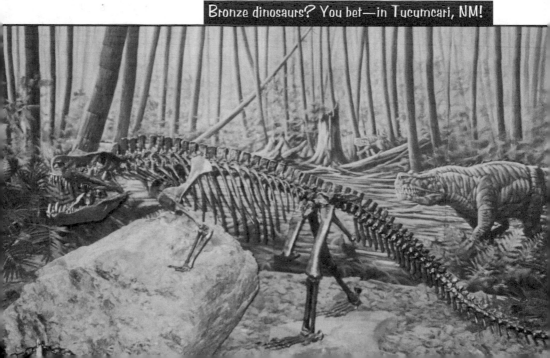

Bronze dinosaurs? You bet—in Tucumcari, NM!

the vertebrae are testament to the enormous size and length of its backbone. This particular creature was 110 feet long (20 feet longer than the distance from home plate to first base on a professional baseball diamond). The oversized vertebrae are a punctuation mark on the creature's length.

If you bring the kids along to this museum, there's a rather large section ("Kids Digs") in the middle of all the displays specifically geared for the little ones. Among other diversions, youngsters are afforded an opportunity to ride an *Apatosaurus,* to view an oddly colored *Stegosaurus,* and to dig for fossils in an enormous sand pit filled with walnut shells and realistically designed paleontological tools. It's a great opportunity for children to get some hands-on experiences with the world of scientific discovery.

Rounding the corner, I move into the Cretaceous period. Here I discover an incredible bronze cast of a *Triceratops* skull that, at first glance, appears to be about twenty times larger than a human head. The display is entitled "Touch a Triceratops" and the authenticity of this cast is sufficient for me to reach out and give it a very gentle pat on the top of its head. Unlike my cat, however, it offers no endearing sound effects or requests for food.

In a nearby corner is a cast of several dinosaur footprints entitled "Dragging its Tail." Many old movies portrayed

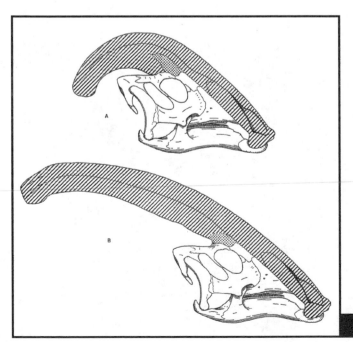

Parasaurolophus skulls

dinosaurs as lumbering, tail-dragging beasts. Yet we know from extensive studies of dinosaur prints (we'll visit some of those in chapter 9) that dinosaurs actually held their tail off the ground. Nevertheless, this rare exception, found in northeastern New Mexico, shows that at least one particular specimen was truly dragging its tail behind. It's not known for certain why the tail was dragging, but there is some speculation that this dinosaur may have been limping.

One of the displays in this section of the museum is called "Tucumcari—Beachfront Property." Here, visitors can view an intriguing display of ancient ammonites, giant oysters, and other marine life that inhabited the seas that ebbed and flowed over this part of the continent millions of years ago. As you might expect, shell collecting is not permitted here.

Two of the most interesting displays in this part of the museum feature dinosaur skin and dinosaur eggs. Here there are the fossilized remnants of skin from a hadrosaur (also known as "duck-billed dinosaurs") and a ceratopsian—most likely a *Triceratops*. Looking remarkably like a collection of skipping stones (rocks young boys [and a few old men] use to skip across the waters of a pond or river in the summertime), these fossils are rare—quite rare—and offer a unique glimpse into body parts not often seen in many museums. In an adjacent display case are various examples of dinosaur eggs, including a theropod egg, an oviraptor egg, a sauropod embryo, and a hadrosaur embryo. There's also a cast of a *T. rex* egg and a sign that states: "A *Tyrannosaurus rex* egg was one of the biggest known eggs. Eggs cannot get too large because: 1. The shell would be too thick for oxygen to seep through to allow the embryo to breathe. 2. The baby could not break through the shell to hatch without a jackhammer."

Nearby is a large fiberglass mold of an *Acrocanthosaurus*—which was the largest carnivore (approximately 40 feet long and 13 feet tall) that lived in New Mexico during the early part of the Cretaceous period (74 to 76 million years ago). This particular sculpture, featured on the Discovery Channel, was made to fit tracks found in central Texas,

The only confirmed *T. rex* track in the world.

showing this prehistoric giant hunting a herd of sauropods. It may well have been the sine qua non of New Mexican predators.

On an adjacent wall is a cast of a *Parasaurolophus* skull, a late Cretaceous dinosaur that lived about 75 million years ago in the Kirkland Formation of northwestern New Mexico. This creature had the most elaborate head adornment of any dinosaur you are likely to encounter—a hollow crest sweeping back from the front of its head (imagine a long, curving trumpet mounted backward on the head of a surrealistic antelope). It is speculated that this oddly formed crest served as a resonance chamber for mating or warning calls. To punctuate the significance of this cranial resonance chamber, the museum curators have—much to the chagrin of parents and certain visiting authors from Pennsylvania—made it possible for kids to produce simulated *Parasaurolophus* sounds simply by pushing a button on the display—that is to say, pushing it over . . . and over . . . and over . . . and . . .

One of the most fascinating displays in this section of the museum is the cast of a *Tyrannosaurus* footprint. This particular footprint is the only confirmed *T. rex* track known anywhere in the world. The actual footprint (measuring 33 inches long by 28 inches wide) is located on the Philmont Boy Scout Camp grounds near Raton, New Mexico. The footprint is on private property, in an inaccessible area, and has been fenced and locked against any would-be pilferers (in case you're considering absconding with a multimillion-year-old and multiton dinosaur track). What is most distinctive about this footprint is the arrangement of three large toes and a fourth smaller toe. The fourth toe (not indicated in any other suspected *T. rex* tracks) is known as a hallux. The only other animals that possess a hallux are modern-day birds—giving further credibility to the dinosaur to bird evolutionary argument.[17]

There's also a dinosaur egg kids can touch. Neat!

Throughout this most unique museum are arranged a collection of posters, murals, and illustrations by artist Paul Koroshetz. They include an enormous variety of scenes, critters and fossils from the Triassic, Jurassic, and Cretaceous periods. In addition, there are lots of visual information for both parents and kids that keeps the interest levels high and the information flowing.

But what is most striking and most distinctive about this museum are its bronze casts. These replicas[18] are not only authentic in every detail but they almost beg you to touch them—to feel their every detail and get an appreciation for their physical size as well as their intricate detail. This is a place unlike any other—and a place perfect for the entire family. There's an abundance of information here about dinosaurs and their times that provides a most complete picture of life in prehistoric times.

NEED TO KNOW

DIRECTIONS From Albuquerque, take I-40 east. Take exit 329 for US 54 E/I-40 BUS/Historical US 66. Merge onto I-4 BUS E/US 54 E/Tucumcari Blvd. and continue to follow I-40 BUS E/W Tucumcari Blvd. Turn left onto S First St. and then take the second right onto Laughlin Ave.

From Albuquerque, the drive is about 175 miles and will take you about 2 hours and 49 minutes.

---

17 You can see a fascinating and absorbing two-minute video of Dr. Spencer Lucas of the New Mexico Museum of Natural History and Science, showing off this one-of-a-kind *T. rex* track at www.youtube.com/watch?v=eGq7FVYDBpM.
18 Almost all the dinosaur displays, in almost all the museums around the world, are replicas—often made of fiberglass. The actual fossils are too precious, and much too fragile, to go on display for the viewing public.

CONTACT INFORMATION Mesalands Community College's Dinosaur Museum, 222 E. Laughlin St., Tucumcari, NM 88401 (575-461-3466; www.mesalands.edu/museum/museum.htm).

FEES Adult (12–64) $6.50, seniors (65+) $5.50, children (5–11) $4, children under 5 free.

HOURS March 1–Labor Day, Tues.–Sat. 10 AM–6 PM; Labor Day– February 28/29, Tues.–Sat. noon–5:00 PM. Closed Sun. and Mon, as well as Thanksgiving, Christmas, and New Year's Day.

BEST TIME TO VISIT All year long.

CAMPING/LODGING For the most up-to-date information about accommodations in Tucumcari, check out the Tucumcari/Quay County Chamber of Commerce website, www.tucumcarinm.com, which also has a complete visitor's guide and event calendar (according to the site, "There is something happening in and around Tucumcari all year round!").

ACCESS The museum is wheelchair accessible.

NOTES The museum may be small, but it's packed with lots of information about dinosaurs in general and about the dinosaurs of New Mexico specifically. It doesn't have the gloss and glitter of big-city museums, but it has a unique charm about it that will provide you with the basics of Southwestern paleontology in a unique, hands-on manner. If you're planning to visit eastern New Mexico, the museum should be on your agenda.

Chapter 9

Footprints in Time

According to information disseminated by New Mexico State Parks (www.nmparks.com), Clayton Lake "is characterized by rolling grasslands, volcanic rocks and sandstone bluffs. Set on the western edge of the Great Plains, it was a stopover point for travelers along the Cimarron Cutoff of the Santa Fe Trail. Visitors today can enjoy picnicking, camping and superb fishing, as well as view one of the most extensive dinosaur trackways in North America."

I'm here for the dinosaurs!

As I drive toward the town of Clayton, eastern New Mexico gives a whole new meaning to the term *flat*. It's possible to drive on straight ribbons of highway and across great stretches of prairie for 30 to 40 miles before encountering any topography or seeing another car. There's plenty of animal company, however—deer, pronghorn antelope, small mammals, scurrying lizards, and birds of every color pass in and out of view along the sleepy back roads.

Clayton Lake State Park

Clayton Lake State Park is 12 miles outside of town via NM 370. Here you'll see some topography and the road does a little weaving in and around two buttes, some very green mesas, stands of trees, wide expanses of grassland, and the ever-present herds of cows contently munching on short tufts of grass. Long lines of barbed-wire fencing parallel the road.

Clayton Lake State Park is a landscape of 471 acres highlighted by a 170-acre lake—it is a picturesque area with expansive and sienna-tinged views in all directions. As I guide my car over the graveled road, the azure waters of the lake rise up to greet me. I pull off onto a dirt road on my right. I enter a small parking area and note a small sign:

> Clayton Dinosaur Trackway—One of the best dinosaur trackways in the world can be viewed at Clayton Lake State Park. More than 500 fossilized footprints made by at least eight kinds of dinosaurs are visible on the lake's spillway. These tracks were embedded in the mud over 100 million years ago when most of New Mexico was a vast sea.

Lathering myself up with sunscreen (a must!), slipping on my dashing safari hat, and fortifying myself with two bottles of authentic spring water, I walk through a gate and down a dirt path that will take me to the spillway. The trail, which borders the edge of the lake, is easy to navigate.

The Clayton Dinosaur Trackway is nothing short of spectacular!

Black swallowtail butterflies, birds chirping in trees, and an occasional lizard greet me at various twists and turns in the trail. I note a series of old tree trunks poking up from the surface of the lake—a confirmation that the lake was not natural.

The area has recently experienced some heavy rains and there are footprints embedded in the soft mud along the trail. Here are recorded the passing of well-shod humanoids in their Nikes and Reeboks. The irony of human tracks temporarily pressed in the earth on the way to see dinosaur tracks that are permanently recorded in stone is not lost on me.

The trail swings around the end of the lake, makes a sharp left, and continues along a ridge leading to the spillway. Glancing up I notice a group of circling vultures in the distance—about 20 of them are hovering over something on the ground. "Be careful not to do anything that might bring me to the attention of a more modern carnivorous species," I tell myself. I walk just a little faster.

At the end of the trail is a small pavilion whose signage informs me that during the construction of the dam no tracks could be seen in the

rock layers. It was only after several years of exposure to rain and snow that the sand layers that filled the depressions were gradually loosened and the compacted surface of each track could be recognized.

I quickly learn that this area was once a beach. It's not certain whether the shoreline belonged to a lake or a marine seaway simply because few traces of other animals or plants have been discovered. It is known, however, that there were forests of hardwood trees and heavy underbrush further inland. It is speculated that this plant material was food for the herbivores that inhabited this environment. Further speculation suggests that the plant eaters may have been crossing a mudflat—moving from one feeding ground to another. It is likely, scientists think, that carnivores were following, looking to pounce on a lone individual, an unprotected baby, or a sick dinosaur separated from the herd.

Before the dinosaurs trampled the surface, the limey mud was soft and gooey. It was deposited by water that may have been brought in by a tide or heavy rainfall. The water evaporated leaving the mud exposed to air. As it gradually dried, mud rocks developed in some places and the ripple marks became hardened. The dinosaurs walked over this surface when the mud was just dry enough to be stiff and just wet enough to be molded by their heavy feet.

The signage in the pavilion also explains, "At least eight kinds of dinosaurs wandered about on this ancient mudflat. All were bipedal (walking on the hind legs only) with both plant-eaters and meat-eaters amongst them. One track was made by a baby dinosaur and another track seems to have been made by a flying reptile (pterodactyl). Meat-eating dinosaurs were here and their tracks are quite common. Characteristically, the carnivores made three-toed tracks. They look very much like a bird's footprint—slender toes and sometimes with claw marks. At this site there are tracks from three kinds of meat-eaters—a heavy-bodied carnivore about the shape and size of an ostrich, a light-bodied carnivore about the shape and size of a sandhill crane or a blue heron, and a puzzling web-toed carnivore that walked on its heels. The most common variety of track was made by dinosaurs that resemble the duck-billed dinosaurs of later times. They are called *Iguanodonts* in reference to their family name Iquanodontidae. There are at least three kinds of *Iguanodont* tracks here. They had broad muscular feet with three blunt toes and the largest of these dinosaurs weighed more than a ton. They probably consumed hundreds of pounds of plants each day. If you follow the boardwalk path you will see some examples of these tracks. One baby dinosaur left its tracks here, too. Because they were so light, baby dinosaurs did not sink far into the mud as they walked and their tracks are not commonly preserved here or anywhere else in the world. The one baby's tracks seems to be from a miniature iguanodont, but paleontologists cannot be confident that it is related to any of the adult-sized dinosaurs."

Another sign is titled "Tracks Demonstrate Dinosaur Behavior": "In some cases, specific examples of behavior can be recognized. At this site a unique example of a tail impression shows where a large plant-eater slipped in the mud and used its tail for balance to keep from falling. In another location we can observe where a dinosaur stepped into a dry puddle that had ripple marks and cracked mudcracks. It then walked on loose sand that did not preserve the impressions of the feet. Fossils bones show dinosaur skeletons, but tracks preserve a record of dinosaur behavior—an instant of time frozen into the rocks. From tracks and trackways it is possible to calculate how much a dinosaur weighed, the way it stood, the way it walked, and how fast it walked. In another example, a different plant-eater hesitated, rocking back and forth until it finally turned to the right and walked into the mud. That sequence of tracks seems to show some form of thinking where the individual was indecisive and had to hesitate before continuing its locomotion. Some of the tracks here form recognizable trackways. It is possible to follow some of the trackways for as many as 20 steps. Such trackways

At least eight kinds of dinosaurs wandered about on this ancient mudflat.

show direction of travel and some can be used to determine velocity."

After filling up on all the signage, I leave the pavilion and walk down a short stairway to the boardwalk to see the tracks. Along the side of the boardwalk is a metal garbage pail with a sign posted over it: "The dinosaurs did not litter. Please follow in their footsteps."

The boardwalk is in a circular pattern—about 220 yards for the complete circle. It encompasses several different sets of footprints recorded in the rock—remnants of different dinosaurs; some large, others small. They are indicators of not only the size of various creatures, but how fast they walked, how they walked (one foot in front of the other signifying an erect gait or a sprawling gait indicating a semierect posture), how many creatures were in a specific spot, which types of animals were predominant in this area, and the direction(s) in which they were headed. It's sort of like taking a census of people in a rural town—just a few facts can reveal a tremendous amount about habits, behaviors, and customs.

It is not unusual for paleontologists to refer to dinosaur tracks as "experiments in soil mechanics." That means that the tracks can also provide scientists with valuable information about the composition of the soil when the tracks were made, as well as the materials that composed that soil in prehistoric times. The ancient geography of an area can be reconstructed depending on whether a creature stepped into mud or sand, or whether it left a deep footprint or a shallow one.

I'm like a kid in a candy store—staring at each set of tracks and letting my imagination drift backward—millions of years in the past— to conjure images of sauropods and theropods ambling through this prehistoric environment. Scenes from *Jurassic Park* flash through my mind as I meander around the perimeter of this visual wonderland.

In my wanderings I note that many of the tracks are clogged with dirt and silt, suggesting that the spillway floods every now and then. Several of the tracks have short grasses and other plants growing inside them. This presents a decidedly surrealistic scene—modern-day plants taking root inside multimillion-year old footprints.

I note that some tracks are widely spaced from each other; whereas others are a little closer together. I later learn that paleontologists have a number of mathematical formulas to calculate the speed of dinosaurs, based primarily on the stride length of the tracks. Although my mathematical ability is severely limited (having never made it past basic geometry in college), I'll see if I can detail this in a way that won't cast any further aspersions on my intellectual capabilities.

If you or I, for example, were to run with wet, bare feet down a dry sidewalk, the distance between each of our footprints would be greater than if we were walking down that same sidewalk with those same soggy feet. In other words, our stride length walking is considerably shorter than our stride length running. The same holds true for dinosaurs.

Surrealistic! Modern-day plants growing inside a multimillion-year-old footprint!

The sauropod (four-legged, herbivorous animals) stride length of the tracks at this site indicate that they were traveling at a speed of about 2 to 4 mph. On the other hand, the stride length of the theropods (often referred to as "beast-footed") shows that they were moving at a speed of about 4 to 6 mph. Both of these speeds indicate that most of the animals were walking rather than running or galloping. It is likely, therefore, that they weren't being chased or that they weren't doing the chasing.

I linger long at each new set of trackways, wondering about the intents or intensions of the creatures that created them. Where were they going? What were they doing? How were they behaving? I find myself asking an array of questions for which there are no easy answers—questions that will undoubtedly continue to exist for several more millennia.

One of the persistent questions I pose to myself is, "Why are there so many different kinds of tracks here?" Even a casual observation of these prints indicates creatures of different sizes and different habits. It is only later, after I return home, that I discover that the Clayton Lake prints are convincing evidence that different species of dinosaurs most likely traveled together in groups. Moreover, these tracks confirm that different age groups of the same species (e.g., adults and juveniles) also traveled in groups—both large and small.

As I near the end of my journey around the 1/8-mile boardwalk, I notice that a family of three has arrived. Mom, Dad, and an eight-year-old boy struggling with an eight-month-old black Labrador puppy begin their prehistoric journey. They are walking the boardwalk and peering intently at the dinosaur tracks. The parents are sharing with their son the information on the numerous posted signs. The young boy is chattering away like a magpie on steroids and can't seem to drink it all in. This is his world.

And then it occurs to me that where this family and I are standing—at 5,176 feet above sea level—used to be underwater: It was once an inland sea!

As I ascend the stairway, I can't help but take one last look at this amazing site. My camera is filled with an abundance of photos that I will later stare at for hours—the geological and paleontological information revealed by these prints is almost beyond the imagination. This is a site that captures the mind and just doesn't let go. It is engaging, it is fascinating, and it is incredible.

It is the perfect place for any eight-year-old—or those who would like to be eight years old again!

▲▼▲▼▲

I saunter back along the trail taking in the vibrant landscape one more time. I climb into my car, slowly wend my way out of the park, and travel back into Clayton. Glancing at the gas gauge I notice the needle creeping toward E. I pull into a Sinclair gas station on the edge of town to fill up. It is only then that I see the iconic company mascot—an *Apatosaurus*—perched on the overhead canopy. "What would he tell me about those tracks and the creatures that made them?" I wonder, as I fill the tank with fossil fuel.

NEED TO KNOW

DIRECTIONS From Albuquerque, head north on I-25. Travel past the exit for Santa Fe and Las Vegas (NM). After about 187 miles make a right hand turn at Exit 412 (in Springer) onto US 412 E/US 56 E/Fourth St. Continue on US 56 E for about 83 miles. As you get into the town of Clayton, keep right at the fork. Turn left onto N. First St., go about 1/2 mile, and turn right onto Clayton Lake Road (NM 370). Travel for about 11 miles and turn left onto State Route 455. Drive about 2.3 miles directly into Clayton Lake State Park. Go through the entrance gate (on your right), pay your fee, and head over to the asphalt parking area on the right. Park your car, grab your camera, and head down the trail to the spillway.

From Albuquerque, the drive is about 285 miles and will take you about 5 hours.

CONTACT INFORMATION **Clayton Lake State Park**, 141 Clayton Lake Rd., Clayton, NM 88415 (575-374-8808; www.emnrd.state.nm.us/PRD/Clayton.htm)

FEES Day use (per vehicle), $5; walk in/bicycle, no charge

HOURS Open 7 days a week; entrance available 24 hours.

BEST TIME TO VISIT Any time during the year—spring, summer, and fall are best. Best time to see the footprints is in the early morning or late afternoon, when the sun casts them in perfect shadows.

CAMPING/LODGING For the latest information on hotels, bed & breakfasts and timeshares in and around Clayton, log on to the Clayton/Union County website, www.claytonnewmexico.net/.

ACCESS The trail from the small parking area to the spillway would be challenging for most wheelchair-bound visitors. Lots of assistance would be necessary. Once at the spillway, there is an overlook to view the footprints. The stairway down from the overlook to the walkway around the footprints is not wheelchair accessible.

NOTES The interpretive signs in the pavilion just above the spillway are thorough and informative (you may need to do a little explaining for younger family members). Be sure to walk down the stairway to the boardwalk that encircles the prints and take your time as you walk around this paleontological wonderland. Be prepared to take lots of photographs and record lots of delightful memories. Just imagining the size of the creatures that left these prints will stimulate all sorts of creative stories and tales.

CHAPTER 10

Of Symbols and Coelophysis

It is well known that state legislators are very busy people. They have laws to pass, committee meetings to attend, bills to draft, constituencies to deal with, and lobbyists to bargain with.

In and among all those official duties, our legislators make sure our state is getting the attention it so richly deserves. States that get a lot of attention are states visited by lots of tourists, thus ensuring a vibrant and robust state economy. One of the best ways to make sure everyone knows about your state (or my state) is to designate certain regional symbols for that state. For example, if you saw a picture of the Alamo on the front of a travel brochure, you would certainly know what state was being "advertised." By the same token, if you saw someone wearing a hat in the shape of a very large piece of cheese (fondly known as a "Cheesehead"), you would undoubtedly know what state that person was representing. The symbols a state has truly separates it from every other state and makes it unique in the eyes of its tourists.

The landscape that inspired Georgia O'Keeffe.

Well, to have state symbols, the legislators have to pass the laws that designate certain objects as those symbols in accordance with the customs, traditions, and/or history of said state. That's why every state has a state bird and a state flower. Almost every state even has an official state insect. Most all states have an official state fish, an official reptile and/or amphibian, and some kind of official food (In my state of Pennsylvania there is an official cookie—the chocolate chip cookie; and an official beverage—milk).

In and among all these official symbols many states have also designated official state fossils (not to be confused with the prehistoric species that frequent the halls of Congress). And, this is where things get really interesting. For example, were you aware that the state fossil of Illinois is a 300-million-year-old worm (*Tullimonstrum gregarium*)? Yes, a worm! Not to be outdone by the folks in the "Prairie State," North Dakota's state fossil is Teredo petrified wood.

Alabama's state fossil is a whale (*Basilosaurus cetoides*); Maryland's is a snail (*Ecphora gardnerae gardnerae*); and Oregon's is a leaf (*Metasequoia*). Delaware's state fossil is an ancient carnivorous squid (*Belemnite*); and in Minnesota, it's a giant beaver (*Casturoides ohioensis*). Virginia may have one of the most distinctive official state fossils—a scallop (*Chesapecten jeffersonius*) named for a former president (who

actually did not serve his country during the Pliocene epoch when this creature was alive).

Fortunately, the good people of New Mexico had the foresight, acumen, and all-around good sense to designate a dinosaur—*Coelophysis*—as their official state fossil.

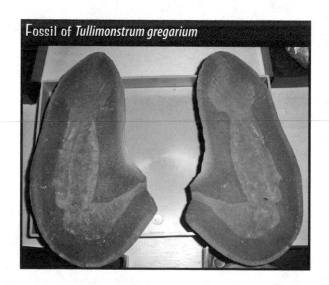

Fossil of *Tullimonstrum gregarium*

Coelophysis fossils were discovered near Abiquiu, NM.

You see, during the early 1980s, there was a concerted effort to build a natural history museum in New Mexico (which we visited in chapter 7). Supporters of the museum initiative campaigned to have the New Mexico State Legislature designate an official state fossil to add to the other state emblems being considered at the time. Some of those

The story behind New Mexico's state fossil.

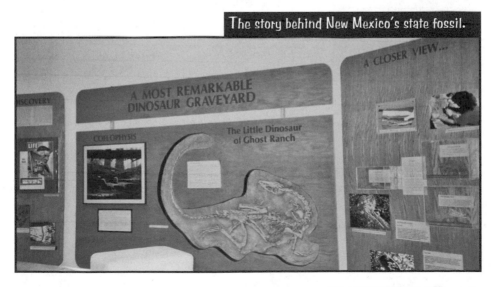

symbols included an official state flower (yucca), state tree (piñon), state animal (black bear), state bird (roadrunner), and two official state vegetables (the chile *and* the pinto bean). It seemed logical, then, that a dinosaur—*Coelophysis*—found almost exclusively in a fossil bone bed at Ghost Ranch in Rio Arriba County should be the fossil designate. Thus, on March 17, 1981, the New Mexico State Legislature officially declared *Coelophysis* the State Fossil. Not only is *Coelophysis* a worthy designate, it is one with a most interesting biography.

But before we explore its life, we need to take a trip.

For readers who may be interested, here is a listing of some of the official symbols for both the "Grand Canyon State" and the "Land of Enchantment."

	Arizona	New Mexico
State Amphibian	Arizona Tree Frog	New Mexico Spadefoot Toad
State Bird	Cactus Wren	Roadrunner
State Reptile	Arizona Ridge-nosed Rattlesnake	Whiptail Lizard
State Fish	Apache Trout	
State Butterfly	Two-tailed Swallowtail Butterfly	Sandia Hairstreak Butterfly
State Insect		Tarantula Hawk Wasp
State Flower	Saguaro Cactus Blossom	Yucca Flower
State Mammal	Ringtail	
State Gemstone	Turquoise	Turquoise
State Tree	Palo Verde	Piñon Tree
State Neckwear	Bola Tie	Bola Tie
State Colors	Blue and Gold	Red and Yellow

State Soil	Casa Grande Soil	
State Aircraft		Hot-air Balloon
State Grass		Blue Grama Grass
State March	Arizona March Song	
State Poem		"A Nuevo Mexico"

▲▼▲▼▲

On this particular venture through the "Land of Enchantment" I intentionally booked a hotel room in Española (just north of Santa Fe). I wanted to take advantage of what *New Mexico Magazine* had designated as the best taco in the state—those served at El Parasol along NM 76 on the way to Chimayó. El Parasol is a taqueria—an unassuming taco stand you may pass by on your way to somewhere else—but please don't!

It has an extensive menu—everything from homemade enchiladas to absolutely the best tacos I've ever eaten anywhere! Having grown up in Southern California, I was weaned on good homemade tacos. Thus, when the restaurant reviewer at *New Mexico Magazine* wrote that the tacos at El Parasol (602 Santa Cruz Road, (502-753-8852) consisted of "corn tortillas crisped on the *plancha,* wrapped around shredded chicken, guacamole, and cool lettuce," I knew I would be in epicurean heaven.

I order four *pollo con salsa* tacos and a Diet Coke. After a short wait (these delights are obviously cooked to order), I retreat to one of the nearby picnic tables, set under a stand of cottonwood trees. Unwrapping my

Absolutely the best tacos in the world! Five stars!

first taco, I discover a homemade tortilla crisped to perfection. Freshly shredded chicken, a hint of cilantro, and a marvelous salsa that kept singing to my taste buds greeted my first bite. I am hooked!

As I eat, trucks and cars pull into the parking area and leave with take-out orders that would feed small armies. It is evident that this local eatery is on everyone's gourmet agenda. By the third taco I decide that the editors of *New Mexico Magazine* may want to re-think their endorsement of this restaurant—they do not serve the best tacos in New Mexico, but the best tacos anywhere in the Southwest! A meal at El Parasol should be on your agenda, too—it offers an exquisite blending of taste sensations that will have you including Española in your travel plans for many years to come.

Next, I head northward on Route 84 for Ghost Ranch. Passing by the quaint village of Abiquiu, I drive through the Kodachromatic geology surrounding Ghost Ranch, with its striking cliffs laced with ribbons of reds, whites, and greens. Clusters of puffy clouds are scattered across the piercing blue skies overhead. This is a sensual and visual wonderland and one can quickly see why Georgia O'Keeffe found this country so startling, so luminescent, and so incredibly rich in color and design.

Driving down a dusty pebbled road, I wind my way through this resplendent landscape to Ghost Ranch. I park in front of the Ruth Hall

The geology around Ghost Ranch is both stunning and spectacular.

Paleontology Museum—a small one-room museum that documents one of paleontology's most spectacular finds—the tiny and enigmatic *Coelophysis*. A new journey into the past has begun!

As I enter the tiny museum I discover a display labeled *Discovery*. It reads: "Paleontologist Edwin H. Colbert from the American Museum of Natural History in New York City made a brief stop at Ghost Ranch in the summer of 1947. He and his field assistants were traveling to the fossil-bearing rocks at the Petrified Forest National Park in northern Arizona when they made a side trip to northern New Mexico. Previous museum and university expeditions in the 1920's and 1930's by the University of California at Berkeley and others had found many fossils in the red and green hills of Ghost Ranch. Shortly after their arrival Colbert and his men made an extraordinary discovery which prompted them to cancel their plans to conduct field work in Arizona. Along the slopes of an arroyo in the spaces of a few tens of yards the paleontologists found bones of what proved to be dozens upon dozens intertwined *Coelophysis* dinosaurs—adults, juveniles, dinosaurs of all ages died together in this deposit which has become one of the most important dinosaur localities in the world."

Beside the display is a copy of the Monday, July 14, 1947, *New York Times* reporting the discovery. There is also a copy of the telegram from E. H. Colbert (dated June 30, 1947) to the American Museum of Natural History, announcing the dinosaur discovery at Ghost Ranch and his request for more help with the excavation. Included is also a copy of the *Life* magazine issue from August 11, 1947—specifically, an article entitled "Earliest Dinosaurs."

Hung on the wall is a small but equally significant display entitled "The Little Dinosaur of Ghost Ranch." Here, visitors can see a cast of an adult *Coelophysis* skeleton excavated shortly after the discovery of the Ghost Ranch dinosaur quarry in 1947. The original fossil (AMNH7224) is on exhibit at the American Museum of Natural History in New York. This skeleton is remarkably complete—the head and neck were drawn back over the body as the muscles tightened after death. The left leg and foot are folded up above the lower back and pelvis. The original right foot was missing and was subsequently restored in this cast. Most of the tail is also a restoration. The skeleton was not found isolated as it is now displayed, but was lying over several others in the same area.

The Ghost Ranch dinosaur quarry is particularly notable because it has revealed the remains of hundreds of whole or partial skeletons. This raises a perplexing question, "Why are so many skeletons found together in one place?" One large block extracted from Ghost Ranch (now on display at the Carnegie Museum of Natural History in Pittsburgh) may have the answer. It shows numerous fish bones embedded below the *Coelophysis* remains. It is speculated that perhaps a large group of *Coelophysis* was attracted to a small pond or lake by an abundance of fresh food and then overwhelmed in a flash flood. The arrangement of the skeletons makes it appear as though the little dinosaurs were swept downriver and dumped where the current slowed. As the skeletons are relatively intact, the animals probably drowned and then were covered up—rather than dying of some cause beforehand.

Additional museum displays provide visitors with information about the Hayden Quarry at Ghost Ranch, which has provided an unusually rich bonanza of Triassic fauna, among them bones of phytosaurs.[19] This particular quarry has produced three genera of dinosaurs—the greatest diversity of any North American Triassic location. Most of the dinosaurs discovered are small predators—each weighing 100 pounds or less.

Although this is a small museum, it contains a treasure trove of information about the discovery of the New Mexico state fossil—*Coelophysis*—and its ultimate impact on the field of paleontology.

---

19 The museum explains, "Phytosaurs are extinct group of late Triassic reptiles. Long-snouted and heavily armored they resemble modern-day crocodiles in size, appearance, and lifestyle. Nevertheless, they are not ancestral to crocodilians. Modern-day crocodiles and alligators always have nostrils at the tip of their snout, while phytosaur nostrils are directly in front of their eyes."

It may be difficult to imagine, but what we now know as the American Southwest (specifically New Mexico) was, in prehistoric times, located much farther south on the planet. In fact, the Ghost Ranch was once at the same latitude as is today's Panama Canal. That meant that this area experienced a climate that was more tropical than

Hands-on paleontology is very much a part of the museum.

desert—warm environment with both wet and dry seasons. Specifically during the Triassic period, the Southwest was a region dominated by vast forests, an abundance of rivers, and significantly elevated levels of humidity.

Museum signage informs me that Pangaea had very few geographical barriers. As a result, animals were free to roam, migrate, and travel great distances across this enormous land mass. This is particularly significant when we consider that different species of *Coelophysis* have been discovered in far-reaching areas of the world. For example, the American species *Coelophysis bauri* is specific to New Mexico (with a few specimens from Arizona), whereas the African species *Coelophysis rhodeniensis* has been discovered in Zimbabwe. It could well be argued that *Coelophysis* wandered far and wide across the prehistoric supercontinent.

The New Mexico state fossil was originally discovered by American paleontologist Edward Drinker Cope in 1887. Cope was particularly taken with the hollow bones of this somewhat incomplete specimen and gave it the scientific name *Coelophysis* ("hollow form"). In Greek, *koilos* means "hollow" and *physis* means "form". At the time, Cope believed that the hollow bones were unique to this critter. However, since the discovery of *Coelophysis*, we know that several other carnivorous dinosaurs also had hollow bones.

Unfortunately, for many years there was only a small collection of poorly preserved fossils. Thus, paleontologists knew very little about *Coelophysis*. Information about its habits, behaviors, lifestyle, appearance, and diet were completely lacking. That is, until the spectacular discovery of a treasure-trove of hundreds of *Coelophysis* skeletons at the Ghost Ranch in 1947.

The Ghost Ranch specimens have revealed an incredible array of information about this late Triassic critter. Perhaps most significant is the fact that the late Triassic was the starting point for the appearance of dinosaurs . . . thus making *Coelophysis* one of the earliest dinosaurs to walk the Earth. That also means that *Coelophysis* would have been at the bottom of the prehistoric food chain (at that time); perhaps spending the better part of its day dodging larger, and more well-established, predatory reptiles such as *Redondasaurus* (26,000 pounds, 39 feet long).

Redondasaurus (model at the Carnegie Museum of Natural History, Pittsburgh, PA)

The Ghost Ranch discoveries have led to interesting speculations about this diminutive dinosaur, based on remains not available to Edward Cope. For one thing, we know that the critter was small and graceful. It was about 10 feet in length and was a little bit more than 3 feet in height. Estimates place its overall weight at about 100 pounds. Given these measurements, it would have been equivalent in size to a modern-day female Great Dane.

It is speculated that *Coelophysis* was an excellent runner. It had long, slender leg bones and would have been able to run in an upright position, much like some modern-day flightless birds such as emus and ostriches. It was also possessed of a long, slender tail that would have functioned as a counterbalance while running. The structure of its bones and its relatively light weight are indicators of a very fast and very agile dinosaur.

Another distinguishing feature of this Triassic critter is short forelimbs with relatively large hands—each with three clawed fingers. This seems to suggest that *Coelophysis* was able to grasp and hold on to its prey—prey that may have included small reptiles and mammals. It is further speculated that this creature lived on the ground rather than in the trees (as other equally small animals did).

Coelophysis's large eyes were positioned about two-thirds of the way along its head. This undoubtedly gave it a distinctive visual advantage: providing it with an extremely large visual field, which would have allowed it to search for both predators and prey throughout a large area, as well as may also have enabled it to locate prey in diminished light; for example, in the early morning before the sun had fully risen.

We also know that it was a carnivorous creature with an array of more than 100 pointed, serrated, teeth—similar, I suspect, to a collection of oral ginzu knives. Each of the teeth showed serrations along the edges —perfect for any meat eater. It is therefore inferred that its relatively strong jaws, in concert with a long and flexible neck and its excellent eyesight, made this short, compact dinosaur a formidable predator in its own right.

In 1982 Carnegie Museum of Natural History paleontologist Dr. David Berman worked with several other institutions to excavate nearly 80 tons of fossil-bearing rock in the *Coelophysis* quarry at Ghost Ranch. Eleven blocks, each weighing up to 4 tons each, were shipped to the Carnegie Museum in Pittsburgh. (An unexpected windfall of these excavations was the discovery of a wealth of spectacular fossils of new or previously poorly known Triassic reptiles. Among them were *Dolabrosaurus* a bizarre, possibly tree-dwelling insectivore and *Hesperosuchus*—a land-living crocodile relative that had been previously known only from fragmentary remains.)

Part of the *Coelophysis* display in the Carnegie Museum is a recording of Dr. Berman's, explaining some of his work with this dinosaur. According to Berman, the *Coelophysis* discovered at the Ghost Ranch provided paleontologists with rich information about the creature's natural history. Prior to the examination of the Ghost Ranch samples, it was unknown how prevalent these creatures were during the Triassic period. Dr. Berman explains that the materials on display clearly indicated that the animals traveled together in large packs and that they were able to survive by working together to attack their prey.

By the way, in the event you'd like to share a little tidbit of trivia with your neighbors, you may wish to mention that *Coelophysis* was the second dinosaur in space. The first dinosaur in space was *Maiasaura*—the "good mother" lizard made famous by paleontologist Jack Horner. However, on January 22, 1998, a *Coelophysis* skull "borrowed" from the Carnegie Museum of Natural History in Pittsburgh was put aboard the Space Shuttle *Endeavor* (Mission STS-89) and taken to the space station Mir. It was subsequently returned to Earth . . . and its rightful place in the museum.

Coelophysis, though small in stature, has contributed greatly to our understanding of the late Triassic environment—particularly in the area we now know as New Mexico. It has rightly earned its place as the state fossil, just as it has earned its place as one of the Mesozoic era's most fascinating animals.

NEED TO KNOW

DIRECTIONS From Albuquerque, head north on I-25. Drive approximately 57 miles. Take exit 282-A/282-B for US 84 N/St. Francis Drive toward US 285 N/Santa Fe Plaza. Merge onto US 285 N/US 84 W/S. St. Francis Drive. Continue to follow US 285 N/US 84 W for about 36 miles. Continue onto US 84 W; after 14.1 miles you will make a right turn onto a dirt road that leads directly into Ghost Ranch (the signage is excellent).

From Albuquerque, the drive is about 109 miles and will take you about 2 hours (depending on the traffic in and around Santa Fe).

CONTACT INFORMATION Ruth Hall Museum of Paleontology, Ghost Ranch, HC 77 Box 11, Abiquiu, NM 87510 (505-685-4333, ext 118; www.ghostranch.org).

FEES Donation.

Ghost Ranch, NM

HOURS Mon.–Sat. 9–5, Sun 1–5.

BEST TIME TO VISIT Any time of the year.

CAMPING/LODGING For information on accommodations, including places to eat and other attractions in the area you may wish to log on to the following website: http://wikitravel.org/en/Abiquiu

ACCESS The museum is handicapped accessible.

NOTES Ghost Ranch in Abiquiu is known worldwide among paleontologists as the location of the articulated fossils of the *Coelophysis,* as well as having one of the richest quarries of the Triassic era. The Ruth Hall Museum of Paleontology is named for amateur paleontologist Ruth Hall, wife of Ghost Ranch director Jim Hall. Displays range from a complete *Coelophysis* cast skeleton to remains from great alligator-like reptiles.

Annually, 2,000 to 3,000 schoolchildren visit the museum on field trips and participate in related educational activities such as the "Dinosaur Bone Dig" and "Plaster Bone Casting," as well as a hike to the *Coelophysis* quarry site.

It is possible to tour the entire museum and read all the displays in about 45 minutes. Although the museum would be considered tiny by most standards, it is set in a landscape where you will want to linger to take in the vistas and sights (polarized sunglasses are strongly recommended) of this dynamic place. An overnight stay in the area is strongly recommended as you will be on sensory overload for quite some time.

ARIZONA

CHAPTER 11
"Your Place for Dinosaurs. . . ."

Grallator footprint

TIME:	Present
PLACE:	Arizona Museum of Natural History, Mesa, Arizona
CHARACTERS:	Jason (Age: 8 years)
	Patrick (Age: 10 years)
	Mother (Age: younger than springtime)
	(opening scene)
JASON:	Mommy, Mommy, look at this!
MOTHER:	*What is it?*

JASON:	It's a dinosaur, a really cool dinosaur!
MOTHER:	*It's called a Pentaceratops. What do you notice about him?*
JASON:	He's got a big head—bigger than mine.
MOTHER:	*Do you notice anything else?*
PATRICK:	Yes, he has one, two, three, four, five horns!
MOTHER:	*What do you think that suggests?*
PATRICK:	Well, maybe he attacked other dinosaurs.
MOTHER:	*What does that mean?*
PATRICK:	Maybe he was protecting his territory.
MOTHER:	*What else do you notice?*
JASON:	Some horns are big and some are short.
MOTHER:	*What do you think that means?*

▲▼▲▼▲

Shortly after entering the Hall of Dinosaurs at the Arizona Museum of Natural History, I find myself following a family of three as they walk past the exhibits and displays. I quickly conclude that this is definitely a place that stimulates lots of question asking and interactions between parents and kids. The three individuals in front of me are obviously engrossed in the dynamic displays sprinkled through this section of the museum. Curiosity is at a fever pitch and interest builds with each

Stegosaurus claims her place on Dinosaur Mountain.

new exhibit and display. As the museum proudly announces on its website, "This is your place for dinosaurs that roar and much more." As evidenced by the enthusiasm of the family in front of me, that is certainly a valid statement.

Strolling into the museum, I was welcomed by a Colombian mastodon on one side of the entry hall and an American mastodon on the other. I paid my admission and immediately headed off to the right and the Hall of Dinosaurs. Inside the hall is the centerpiece of the museum—the spectacular Dinosaur Mountain—a multistory realistic display of various prehistoric creatures (some of which even roar) from the Mesozoic era, soaring from the basement all the way into the third floor. Perhaps one of the most spectacular events is the flash flood that occurs every 23 minutes. This aquatic cascade sends volumes of water barreling down into a large pool at the bottom of the mountain.

The Mountain is organized into four separate zones:

Triassic Arizona (245–205 million years ago)—The base of the mountain displays plants and animals that inhabited the late Triassic period of Arizona (approximately 225 million years ago). Three-dimensional life-size models of *Coelophysis* and *Tanystropheus* are displayed. The latter was a 20-foot long reptile with a neck that was longer than its body and tail combined. Juveniles had three-pronged teeth and adults one-pronged-teeth, which may indicate a change of diet from youth to maturity.

Jurassic Arizona (205–144 million years ago)—The second level from the bottom of the mountain represents life forms from the Jurassic period (about 155 million years ago). Although most of the best-known dinosaurs lived in the Jurassic, few of them have been found in Arizona. Along with *Stegosaurus,* the display includes *Fruitachampsa,* a four-footed predator about 3 feet in length, with a short face and a very distinctive pair of canine-type teeth in its lower jaw; and *Echinodon,* which, at only about 3 feet long, is one of the smallest known dinosaurs; its fossils have not only been discovered in Arizona, but in Portugal and England.

Cretaceous Arizona (144–65 million years ago)—Most of the creatures that inhabited what is now Arizona in the Cretaceous period have been located in the southeastern portions of the state. *Tyrannosaurus rex* is displayed here; however, the museum's website is quick to point out, "In Arizona, we have found fragments of bone

Pentaceratops also has a place on Dinosaur Mountain.

from animals belonging to the tyrannosaur family, but we do not have enough to be sure of their specific identity." The specimen on display (which makes its presence known with periodic roars) is a juvenile. Other dinosaurs in this portion of the Mountain are: *Pentaceratops, Paleosaniwa,* and *Alphadon.*

Cenozoic Arizona (65–1.8 million years ago)—The top layer of the Mountain represent that period of time after the demise of the dinosaurs—the Cenozoic period. A single representative of that time is positioned in this zone: *Glyptotherium*. A distant relative of the sloth and armadillo, *Glyptotherium* migrated to the Southwest from South America shortly after the Panamanian land bridge first appeared. These herbivorous creatures lived in warm climates with lush tropical or subtropical vegetation and proximity to standing water.

▲▼▲▼▲

Dinosaur Mountain is a dynamic display with dinosaurs in lifelike poses and a realistic environment. Its unique presentation draws both kids and parents like chocoholics are drawn to Hershey, Pennsylvania. Every time a new group of kids or a family comes around the corner and see this spectacular construction, there is a chorus of oohs and ahs. However, it is when the "every-23-minutes" flash flood occurs that cameras and cell phones are brought out, small gangs of kids congregate around the railing, and everything else in the museum comes to a virtual standstill as this Mesozoic wonderland comes to life. This is what a museum should be—engaging, dynamic, and realistic.

Dinosaur Mountain is certainly the most commanding display in the Hall of Dinosaurs—but not the only one. Along the walls of this easy-to-navigate museum are numerous display cases, lighted signs, murals, visual representations, and informational signs that are engaging and informative.

As I wend my way through the lower level of the museum I come upon an old friend—*Dilophosaurus* (the frilled, spitting dinosaurs from *Jurassic Park*). A three-dimensional model of this critter is posed in a realistic Jurassic environment—the edge of a prehistoric forest with a small stream, an articulated skeleton of long-dead dinosaur, and a layer of hardened sandstone beneath.

As you may recall from chapter 4, *Dilophosaurus*'s most distinguishing feature is the two crests on its head. It seems, however, that this Arizona dinosaur is not the only one with such a feature. Several new dinosaurs—all with double crests—have been recovered from China. Although it was originally thought that they were *Dilophosaurus,* they have since been reclassified.

I learn later that the discovery and naming of *Dilophosaurus* was

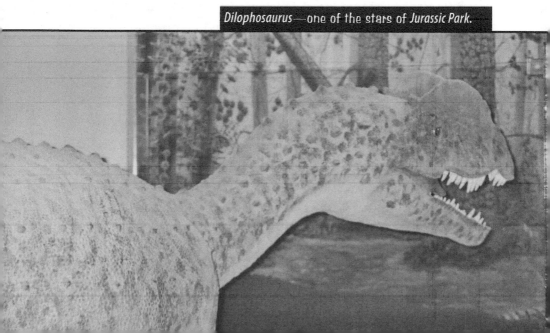

Dilophosaurus—one of the stars of *Jurassic Park*.

filled with some interesting twists and turns. This previously unknown dinosaur was first discovered by Sam Welles, a professor at the University of California Museum of Paleontology, in the summer of 1942. Welles had been previously alerted to the possible presence of dinosaur fossils in the Tuba City area by the owner of a trading post in the area. Sufficiently intrigued, Welles journeyed to the area, and shortly after setting up camp he and his associates began excavating.

In short order they discovered three dinosaurs in a 20-foot area (although one of the specimens had been almost entirely eroded). The second skeleton showed everything except the front part of the skull. However, it was the third specimen that gave them that missing skull part. This was a fossil-rich area; after only ten days of excavation, the specimens were driven back to Berkeley.

The specimens were cleaned and eventually displayed as a single wall mount at UC Berkeley. Eventually, in 1954, Welles published a preliminary description, naming the creature *Megalosaurus wetherilli*. But for some reason, something just didn't seem right about the specimen. It was almost two decades later that Welles began seriously rethinking the age of the specimen he had collected—specifically, he began questioning the type of rock (Triassic or Jurassic) in which the specimen was located. Not satisfied with his answers, he decided to return to the site of the original discovery in northeastern Arizona. There, about a quarter-mile south of the original find, he discovered a fourth skeleton—an almost complete specimen of an adult *Dilophosaurus*.

Back at Berkeley, as this new fossil was being extruded from the surrounding rock, it was discovered that the specimen clearly had a double crest on the top of the head. It was obvious that a new and different name was needed and thus it was officially designated as *Dilophosaurus* ("two-crested lizard"). Later, Welles acknowledged, "The original skull also shows the crest, but we had not recognized it. The two crests had been crushed together, and we had assumed they were part of a cheek bone that had been pushed out of place."

Signage near the museum's 4 1/2-foot-tall, 20-foot-long, and half-ton *Dilophosaurus* informs me that this area (the Kayenta formation) of northeastern Arizona has also revealed an eclectic and varied collection of fossils from the early Jurassic period. These include animals such as the first North American turtle, the first North American mammal, and the first frog.

According to the museum, there have also been other, admittedly less famous, dinosaurs unearthed in the Kayenta Formation. These include *Scutellosaurus,* an armored dinosaur with bony scutes (scales) embedded in its skin; *Syntarsus,* a small (60- to 70-pound), lightly built dinosaur that walked on two long legs; *Massospondylus,* which had large, five-fingered hands with a large thumb claw; *Scelidosaurus,* a 440- to 550-pound dinosaur with tricorns (small, three-pronged horns) behind its ears; and *Heterodontosaurus,* a small, lightly built dinosaur with three different kinds of teeth and a beak.

Walking through the display areas, I am delighted to come upon some information that verifies data I had collected on another venture (Great minds thinking alike!), specifically regarding dinosaur track sites (see chapter 12). A display of dinosaur tracks and an accompanying sign informs me that the Southwest is noted for an abundance of track sites, particularly in the Kayenta Formation. The sign tells visitors, that the tracks on display are indicative of not only different species of dinosaurs, but also of how they may have traveled—running or walking.

▲▼▲▼▲

JASON: Look at this, look at this.

MOTHER: *What do you see?*

JASON: Oh, boy, it's another dinosaur.

MOTHER: *What looks different about him?*

JASON: He's smaller than the other dinosaurs here.

MOTHER: *What do his feet look like?*

PATRICK: They look like Dad's feet!

JASON: No, they look thin. They look narrow.

MOTHER:	*What does that suggest?*
PATRICK:	Maybe it had a tough time walking.
JASON:	Come here. I want to show you something. What's this?
MOTHER:	*It's a Stegosaurus tail spike. What does it remind you of?*
PATRICK:	It looks like a sword or a very long knife
JASON:	Mommy, Mommy, look at this!

▲▼▲▼▲

In the adjacent Hall of Dinosaurs, there are several articulated skeletons of various dinosaurs, including *Probactrosaurus,* a herbivorous dinosaur, principally from China, with an elongated lower jaw and double rows of flattened cheek teeth; *Tenontosaurus,* a 21- to 26-foot-long dinosaur with an unusually long, broad tail; *Iguanodon,* discovered in 1822, this dinosaur was the second dinosaur formally named, after *Megalosaurus; Triceratops,* with its characteristic three horns; and *Tyrannosaurus bataar,* a type of tyrannosaur from Mongolia.

Triceratops

Coming up into the Hall from a lower level, it is necessary to walk between the legs of an enormous *Apatosaurus* (originally known as *Brontosaurus*) to get into the Hall. This creature's legs straddle the

An early depiction of *Apatosaurus*

stairway like a bow-legged cowboy. The term *Apatosaurus* comes from the Greek names *apate,* meaning "deception" and *sauros* meaning "lizard"—thus, "deceptive lizard."[20] *Apatosaurus* lived during the latter part of the Jurassic period, about 157 to 146 million years ago, and their fossils have not only been found in Arizona, but also in Colorado, Utah, and Wyoming.

To say that this creature was large would truly be an understatement. It was gargantuan! It had an average length of about 75 feet, with at least one specimen reaching a length of 85 feet. It is estimated that its total weight was somewhere in the neighborhood of 24 to 32 tons, which would be equivalent to the weight of 128 giant squids, 4 elephants, 19 male giraffes, or 11,200 Chihuahuas (although the thought of trying to line up that many Chihuahuas seems, at best, exasperating).

---

20 The dinosaur was originally named by paleontologist Othniel Charles Marsh. Marsh thought that the creature's chevron bones (bones on the underside of the tail) were similar to those of some mosasaurs (prehistoric marine lizards).

It has been determined that, at most, an *Apatosaurus* could only hold its head up about 17 feet off the ground. If it raised its head any further, its heart would not have been able to pump blood to the head, which, as you might expect, would have had a significantly adverse effect on its life expectancy. It is speculated that this creature held its neck toward the ground—spending most of its days feeding on low plant life rather than foliage high up in Jurassic trees. The tail, on the other hand, may have been used as a giant counterweight. The skeleton of the long neck was extremely light, made of narrow strips and sheets of bone. These supported the neck just as steel beams and sheets hold up a bridge.

The huge body of an *Apatosaurus* needed constant feeding; as a result, the animal must have spent most of its time eating. Its teeth were narrow and peglike, arranged like a comb along the jaws. The tiny head could swing about, allowing it to feed on low vegetation or stretch up to eat from the tops of prehistoric trees. The hips of this dinosaur were very heavy, and the hip muscles were strong enough to allow it to rear up on its hind legs for short periods. There was no time for chewing—the food was just swallowed as quickly as it was plucked. Once it reached the digestive system, the food may have been ground down by gastroliths (stomach stones) the creature swallowed from time to time.

▲▼▲▼▲

During my visit to the museum, a temporary (and traveling) exhibit had been set up in a large hall just off the main lobby. This exhibit—entitled "*Therizinosaur*: Mystery of the Sickle-Claw Dinosaur"—provided information, fossils, displays, illustrations, and stories about one of the Southwest's most enigmatic dinosaurs. You may recall our discussion of this fascinating creature back in chapter 4.

There is, however, more to the story.

When it was first discovered, scientists realized that this dinosaur was out of place. It had been buried in mud that had built up on the bottom of the sea. But most surprising was the fact that it was discovered in a place that would have been 60 miles from the nearest shoreline. A

Therizinosaur

terrestrial dinosaur 60 miles out to sea! How could that be? How did a land-living dinosaur get so far from land amidst the shells of oysters and ammonites, and among skeletons of fish and plesiosaurs?

Although many explanations are possible, the museum proffers two hypotheses—either of which is possible. The first theory suggests that after the dinosaur died it was eventually washed into the ocean, perhaps by a flood. The formation of gases within the decaying carcass allowed the creature to float upward on the surface of the sea. The carcass may have been pushed further offshore by prevailing winds or currents. Eventually it would have decayed and sank to the bottom of the inland sea, belly up. Over time, sediment and debris would have covered the body and the fossilization process would have started. Although this is certainly a plausible explanation, it doesn't answer another question; that is, wouldn't the decaying carcass have been scavenged by various predators (marine or avian) on its 60-mile journey across the sea?

The second theory is that the creature may have been washed out to sea when it was alive. It may have been injured and thus unable to swim back to shore or defend itself. Predators such as sharks and plesiosaurs may have attacked it (interestingly, most of the skeleton fell to the bottom of the shallow sea). This, of course, generates several other, presumably unanswerable, questions. For example, would the creature have been able to defend itself? What forces of nature were at work to push it 60 miles from shore? Was it able to latch on to any floating debris being carried out to sea?

This unique display (which will travel around the state) provides as many questions as it does answers. Such is the way of science. Seldom do scientists find all the answers they need. Often, instead of answers, more questions are generated. That may be one of the endearing realities of paleontology. It's both a science without end and a science without limits.

▲▼▲▼▲

JASON:	Mommy, Mommy, look at this!
MOTHER:	What do you see, Jason?
JASON:	It's a claw! It's a claw! This dinosaur has a claw!
MOTHER:	What are some other animals that have claws?
JASON:	Cats have claws.
PATRICK:	Bears have claws.
JASON:	Tigers have claws.
PATRICK:	Our teacher, Mrs. Rumsey, told us that crabs and lobsters have claws.
MOTHER:	What does this dinosaur remind you of?
JASON:	A great big bird.
PATRICK:	A great big bird with claws.
JASON:	Wow! That's cool!
PATRICK:	Yeah, that's really cool!
MOTHER:	Come on over here—I want to show you something else!

NEED TO KNOW

DIRECTIONS From the Phoenix Sky Harbor International Airport, head east on E. Sky Harbor Blvd. Keep right at the fork and follow the signs for AZ 202 E and merge onto E Sky Harbor Blvd. Keep left at the fork, follow the signs for AZ 202 Loop E/Tempe/Mesa and merge onto AZ 202 Loop E. Take exit 13 for Country Club Drive. Turn right onto N. Country Club Drive. Turn left onto W. Main St. Turn left onto Macdonald. The museum will be on the right.

From the airport, the drive is about 13 miles and, depending on traffic, will take you about 20 minutes.

CONTACT INFORMATION Arizona Museum of Natural History, 53 N. Macdonald, Mesa, AZ 85201 (480-644-2230; http://azmnh.org)

FEES Adults $10, seniors (65+) $9, children (3–12) $6, children 2 and younger free.

HOURS Tues.–Fri. 10–5, Sat. 11–5, Sun 1–5.

BEST TIME TO VISIT Any time of the year. If you're visiting in the middle of July and need a place that is both educational and air-conditioned, this would be the ideal spot.

CAMPING/LODGING Literally thousands of accommodations are available in the greater Phoenix area—everything from dirt cheap all the way up to *"You've got to be kidding me!"* You might want to check out the Arizona Office of Tourism at www.arizonaguide.com.

ACCESS All areas of the museum are handicapped accessible.

NOTES If this is your first visit to the Grand Canyon State and you want to get a flavor for the history, culture, and paleontology of this spectacular state, then the Arizona Museum of Natural History is a great place to start. Be prepared, though, once you get started on your tour of this museum you will be entranced for many hours . . . particularly when you take the kids to see Dinosaur Mountain.

CHAPTER 12
Makin' Tracks

Dinosaur tracks have been found on all the continents except Antarctica. Depending on location, they may range in age from the Triassic period (225 million years ago) to the close of the Cretaceous (65 million years ago). Tracks (also known as trace fossils) are of great interest to scientists because they represent the behavior of the living animals and present information that cannot be derived from skeletons alone. Altogether there may be several hundred trackways in the Southwest, but not all have been studied. One of the most famous is located in northeastern Arizona. My prehistoric Southwestern journeys would not have been complete without a visit to a site just outside Tuba City.

Grand Canyon—North Rim

The dinosaur tracks outside Tuba City, AZ, lure visitors from all over the world.

My morning flight arrives in Phoenix a few minutes ahead of schedule. After grabbing my bags, I get on board the airport's rental car shuttle. Possessed of a car, I then traverse the greater Phoenix metropolitan area and head north on Interstate 17.

Shortly outside Phoenix, the highway is reduced to two lanes, the traffic around me thins considerably, and I'm speeding (excuse me, I'm proceeding at the posted speed limit) on my way to a place three and a half hours distant—a place just west of Tuba City.

Saguaros sprinkle the side of the highway as I head northward. I zip by Cordes Junction (the home of Arcosanti—an experimental town in the high desert committed to lessening humans' impact on the Earth). Shortly after, I pass by Exit 268—an extended dirt road heading westward to the Orme School, the college-preparatory boarding school where I spent five incredible years learning about Greek philosophers, the anatomy of reptiles and amphibians, Spanish verbs, Aztec and Incan civilizations, the differences between declarative and interrogative sentences, and the beauty of the late Miocene, early Pliocene basalt flows of this rugged landscape. Over the last five million years or so, the geological formations of this high desert land has been dissected into rim-rocked mesas, punctuated by expansive views over vast public lands covered with steppe grassland and piñon-juniper savanna. This is a broad landscape—one I traversed on foot (as a former long-distance runner on the school's track team) and on horseback many times during my secondary education. It was like coming home.

The miles pass quickly beneath my wheels and the elevation rises to 7,000 feet. Now the road is bordered by stands of sweet-smelling trees and the constant litter of pine needles. A 70 mph swing around the southern suburbs of Flagstaff, a quick left onto Route 89, and a decent into the high desert of northern Arizona are like a high-definition video—rich, revealing, and remarkable. Here the mountains disappear; the vegetation gets a little scruffier; the road, a little straighter; the sky, a little bluer; and the temperature, a little warmer.

About 67 miles outside of Flagstaff and 14 miles north of Cameron, I make a right-hand turn on Route 160. Hills and buttes and mesas are striated with ribbons of reds and ochres, browns and siennas, and several shades of black. The primordial stripes through these mountains are just incredible—it's a geographical palette of colors that would amaze and delight any artist. The land here is vast and open and wide and stretches as far as the eye or the imagination can go. Valleys, arroyos, gulches with outcroppings of red rock mesas, clusters of hills, and a deep blue horizon that hugs the geology of this area are part of every vista.

After about 4 1/2 miles, there are two hand-lettered signs by the side of the road: "Dinosaurs Tracks—Turn Now." I make a left turn onto a short gravel road with a small pavilion and a phalanx of out-of-state cars parked across the dusty terrain. Just before pulling into the parking area, I am greeted by a young boy of 10 or 11. He waves me over to a parking space. As I exit my car, he introduces himself as Meshach and informs me that he will be my guide over and through the dinosaur tracks positioned a few yards in front of the now-baking vehicles.

After donning my hat and grabbing my recorder, Meshach leads me through a line of six to eight wooden stands each with an array of tables displaying a varied collection of handmade jewelry—bracelets, earrings, pendants, rings, and so on. I quickly get a sense that there's a connection between all this jewelry and the guided tour I'm about to take.

Little did I know.

Before setting out on this venture I had done some reading about the tracks and the Navajo guides who lead visitors through this prehistoric outpost. I learned that the tracks at this site were formed in the early Jurassic period, about 202 to 200 million years ago. Based on the age

Meshach—my paleontological guide.

of the rocks and the fossils of dinosaurs in the area, it's likely that animals such as *Coelophysis* (small tracks) and *Dilophosaurus* (large tracks) made the stony footprints here.

At least two well-versed individuals, each of whom have visited the site on many occasions, advised (warned) me that much of the information shared on my tour of the tracks would be erroneous. A paleontologist acquaintance e-mailed me several weeks in advance of this trip and told me, "The Tuba City track site is really neat, but remember that all of the information that the 'guides' give you there will be wrong." He also said to just smile and nod when presented with some of the obviously fictitious data.

I do a lot of smiling and nodding that day.

Meshach, using his best 10-year-old voice of paleontological authority, begins our trek across the dinosaur track site by telling me that most of the tracks are those of a *Lapasaurus,* which until that point in my education is a dinosaur I have never encountered.[21]

---

21 Intensive Googling revealed that there is no *Lapasaurus* dinosaur.

"Here are baby dinosaur tracks—it's walking with its mother. And this is a seashell. This was a swamp. This was a swamp because this was a sea creature," my young guide proudly informs me.

I can tell he's just getting warmed up—not difficult when the ambient temperature is inching toward triple digits. "This is the footprint of a sea creature," he says with paleontological confidence. "Here is a pterodactyl track that got stuck in the mud and jumped out about ten feet. This is where a pterodactyl apparently took off—there's some foot slippage in the rock."

Already I know I'm in for quite a ride.

"This print is a male and that print is a female 'cause it's all messed up," Meshach tells me with a decided note of authority. "See it's all messed up here. And this is the male 'cause it's not all messed up."

So much for sexual dimorphism, I think to myself.

"And this is a duckbill track."

"How do you know it's a duckbill?" I ask.

"They call it a duckbill because its feet is similar . . . just like a duck. That's why they call it a duckbill," my expert informs me.

As we approach each of the tracks, Meshach pours water from his water bottle into selected tracks so that they stand out against the parched, rust-colored landscape. The watered dinosaur tracks are a constant reminder that millions of years ago, when the dinosaurs walked over this formerly muddy surface, their feet sank into the layers of clay and silt. Where the mud was stiff, the depressions kept their shape, actually showing their anatomy at the bottom of the foot. As the mud dried, dust may have blown over the surface, filling in some of the depressions and later, perhaps as the tide (from the Western Interior Seaway) flooded the surface, fine layers of sand filled each track burying them for the millennia. Over the millions of years since the tracks were made, the mud changed to mudstones and the sands to sandstones.

"These right here are raptor footprints," Meshach announces.

"How do we know that's a raptor?" I inquire of my young paleontologist.

"'Cause these are the deepest prints and a whole bunch of raptors here have a bunch of weight on them and when they step into the mud they go deep . . . way down deep."

Water poured into a a dinosaur track helps it stand out.

Just ahead in the rock I spot a small track. Meshach pours some water into it for relief. Of course, I want to know what kind of dinosaur made the imprint.

"What do the scientists think that is?" I inquire.

"They don't know the name of it or how it's shaped or how it looks and the fact that they can't find the DNA . . . they can't find out 'cause most scientists have too much work to do." They probably work for some governmental bureaucracy, I surmised.

"And here we have a dinosaur that laid down 'cause all the mud was pushed together here."

My curiosity was escalating with the temperature. "Do we know what kind of dinosaur laid down there? I asked.

"No, but it could have been a raptor that laid here."

I was smiling—both for the inventiveness of my guide's responses as well as for the creativity that he injected into every aspect of my tour. I was curious to know where he learned all his paleontology. "So, how do you know so much about dinosaurs, Meshach?"

With the straightest face he replied, "I watch a cartoon program named *Littlefoot*. There are also some scientists who come around here and tell us stuff and I learn lots of things about dinosaurs."

"Have you talked to any of the scientists?" I ask.

"No, we don't really talk to any of them, but we learn stuff from them."

Not wishing to press the "extremely busy scientist" or "nonverbal scientist" angles, I am guided over to a small mound of sandstone with a circle of stones set around it. "What's this?" I ask innocently.

"This is a pteradactyl wing. It's a pteradactyl wing—some parts are hollow [he knocks on it] and some parts are not. You see this big meteor just came flying into the Earth over there [as he points eastward] and all these parts started flying and you can go over to Meteor Crater to learn all about that. And the meter wiped out all the dinosaurs here in Arizona and all the way into Canada."

"Unbelievable," I think to myself.

After that scientific explanation I was shown a *Lapasaurus* head.

"Look the eye socket is here," my scientist friend explains. "My mom

Meteor Crater, 43 miles east of Flagstaff

found a dinosaur head. She took it to one of the scientists that came around here and she asked them what it was and they said 'dinosaur feet,' and this guy said, 'This is worth a lot,' and my mom said, 'How much?' And he said a couple of million. But she wanted to leave it here. But some people have gotten rich.

Shortly afterward we walk around a crest of sandstone and a scattering of rocks. Meshach indentifies one of the larger rocks as the head of a pterodactyl. Even before I can ask the question, Meshach, with all the seriousness of a seasoned paleontologist gives me the answer I need.

"When the meteor hit, everything from the dinosaurs all splattered. When it hit the dinosaur, all its parts went splattered all over the place. And so its head just bounced around until it landed over here." This is certainly a new theory—one I have never encountered before (obviously, I need to get out more!).

Next I am introduced to a cache of five or six "dinosaur eggs" embedded in the rock face. My guide's scientific explanation leaves absolutely nothing to the imagination.

"When it rains and blows it puffs up more. And there was this dinosaur's egg in the bushes and for two days It hatched before the other eggs and the mother got all the other eggs to hatch, too. But then something happened to them. And the mother only wanted two of them so she left the other out here and this is what they look like. When someone else touches the eggs—just like when someone touches a bird egg—the mom doesn't want the egg so maybe someone touched these eggs, too."

We continue our walk, and after a few steps, Meshach bends over and picks up a small red rock. After a quick examination, he hands the rock to me and says, "This is a piece of fossilized dinosaur skin. You can keep it."

"Are you sure," I ask.

"Yeah," there's plenty of that stuff all over here ," he replies authoritatively.

Stuffing it into my pocket, I thank him profusely.

Satisfied he has given me a crash course in the paleontology of this region and the dinosaurs that walked across the landscape, Meshach quickly changes the subject and begins talking about his horse . . . his very, very sick horse.

"You see I'm trying to raise some money—as much as I can so I can take care of my sick horse. We do roundups—that's what I do with my horse. I got my horse from my dad when I was first born, but I had to wait until I was six months and then the horse became mine and I ride my horse a lot . . . and I go on these roundups. "

I see the next part of the story coming from about a mile away, but I am intrigued nonetheless—after all, I am in the hands of an expert.

"But, you see, my horse is really sick now. He needs this shot from the doctor that costs about eighty-nine dollars and I'm trying to raise some money so that he can get the shot and get all better. Then I'll be able to go on the roundup, which is about fifty miles long, and my horse needs to be all better in order so that he can make it all the way. But the shot costs a lot of money and I hope I can get him better soon so that I can go on the roundup with my dad and grandfather."

He is on a roll.

"I hope I can get the money real soon so that I can get that shot. I really care for my horse and get really upset when he gets sick and this ride is important in my family and I don't want to miss it this year, but I have to get the money soon or my horse won't have time to get better. He's really a neat horse and I care for him a lot."

As he shares the perils of horse-raising with me, I realize that the official tour is over and I am deftly and professionally being guided over to one of the jewelry stands at the edge of the parking area. In short order I am presented with an array of jewelry created by his mother (who isn't at the stand, because she is leading another group of tourists through the dinosaur track site). I see necklaces with "turquoise from the bottom of the Grand Canyon," earrings with "petrified wood stones that came from around here," rings with "stones having come from Alaska," and bracelets with "real 24-karat silver" all over them.

I am certain my wife's jewelry collection doesn't need any more knickknacks or bric-a-brac and politely decline making any purchases.

▲▼▲▼▲

Was this venture worth it? Absolutely! Not only did I get to see some of the most impressive dinosaur tracks anywhere in the Southwest, but I also had the opportunity to view them in the context of a dramatic and rich environment.

There may be those who say that this is nothing more than a hustle—a chance for Native Americans to sell inexpensive jewelry to unsuspecting white men, rather than promote scientific accuracy or paleontological research. My guide shared the most rudimentary, if often inaccurate, scientific information about the trace fossils of this area. His horse story went on and on and on—I learned everything there was to learn about a sick horse, a young boy's desire to ride that horse in an annual family pilgrimage, and how important it was to get the sick horse valuable medication. And I also got a salesman's pitch for inexpensive jewelry—a way in which my young guide's family was trying to support itself in tough economic times. Was I taken advantage of? Perhaps. But I had done my homework beforehand. I knew what to expect and what not to trust. I was armed with information about the tracks and what they represented. I enjoyed the journey simply because my guide was eager, ambitious, and fun to be with for 30 minutes on a sweltering summer day in northeastern Arizona. Much of what I "learned" was misplaced information, but it was shared in a spirit of genuine sincerity and interest.

For those traveling to the North Rim of the Grand Canyon, this is certainly a recommended stop. The side trip off Route 89, the tour through the dinosaur tracks, and the return trip to the highway will take all of one hour. It's an important venture in terms of Southwestern paleontology—but a venture one needs to approach with eyes wide open in both the literal and figurative sense. Much of the information on site may be fictitious, but the tracks and the creatures that left them millions of years ago are not.

▲▼▲▼

The dinosaur tracks outside of Tuba City are visited by thousands of tourists every year. Depending on the experience, age, or knowledge of the guide who leads you through this site, you may get lots of misinformation, misinterpretations, or misrepresentations. The following chart outlines some of the "research" frequently shared by the guides, along with the actual truth.

What you may hear	The truth
"These are raptor tracks."	The larger tracks are called *Eubrontes* and were made by a large theropod dinosaur, probably *Dilophosaurus*.
"These are pterodactyl tracks."	Pterodactyls are more properly known as pterosaurs. They are not dinosaurs. There are no pterosaur tracks here.
"This is a pterodactyl wing."	No evidence of pterosaurs (or pterodactyls) has been found here.
"These are baby dinosaur tracks."	The smaller tracks are grallator and most likely made by a dinosaur such as *Coelophysis*.
"Here are some *T. rex* tracks."	The tracks here were made about 135 million years *before T. rex* ever walked the Earth.
"Here are some dinosaur eggs."	The "eggs" are just iron concretions in the sandstone. No eggs from the Jurassic are known in North America.
"This is dinosaur poop."	Fossilized dinosaur poop (known to scientists as coprolites) is quite rare. These, too, are simply iron concretions.
"This is a dinosaur skeleton."	It's a weathered chunk of sandstone.

"A duckbill dinosaur had feet similar to a duck."	Duckbills (also known as hadrosaurs) had "standard" dinosaur feet. They were called duckbills because of their long, flat snouts.
"Here is a place where a dinosaur laid down."	No.
"This is a dinosaur claw."	No. But it is some kind of fossil—most likely a plant or invertebrate.
"Some scientists stole some of the dinosaur skeletons."	Not true.
"The meteor that made Meteor Crater wiped out all the dinosaurs."	Meteor Crater was created just 50,000 years ago—well after the demise of the dinosaurs (65 million years ago).
"This is the head of a pterodactyl."	It's a rock.
'This is the head of a *Lapasaurus* (?)."	It's a rock.
"Here is some fossilized dinosaur skin."	It's a rock.
'Here's a dinosaur bone."	It's a rock.
"This is a rock."	It's a rock!

▲▼▲▼▲

Oh, by the way, before climbing back into my rental car and leaving the Tuba City dinosaur track site, I slipped Meshach a five-dollar bill to help with the expenses of his (very) sick horse.

I know, I know—as P. T. Barnum said, there's one born every minute!

NEED TO KNOW

DIRECTIONS From Phoenix, head north on I-17 (Black Canyon Highway) toward Flagstaff. Just outside Flagstaff, take exit 340A to merge onto I-40 toward Albuquerque. Take exit 201 toward US 89 N/ Page. Turn left onto Country Club Drive. Take the second right onto US

89N. Travel for about 62 miles and turn right onto US 160 E/Navaho Trail. Drive for about 4.6 miles and look for the hand-lettered "Dinosaur Tracks" signs along the right side of the road. Turn left where indicated.

From Phoenix, the drive is approximately 215 miles and will take you about 3 hours and 45 minutes (depending on your inclination to put your "pedal to the metal").

FEES Donation (suggested: $5 to $10).

HOURS Daylight. There is no nighttime outdoor lighting out here.

BEST TIME TO VISIT Any time of the year. Keep in mind that even though this is considered high desert, it can still get pretty hot during

Dinosaur head? No, it's a rock!

the summer. There is absolutely *no* shade, so be sure to bring a head covering and lots (and I mean *lots*) of water! Fifteen minutes in the summer sun will literally fry your brain.

CAMPING/LODGING For information about accommodations (as well as articles about Tuba City), log on to the following website: www.arizonaguide.com/places-to-visit/northern-arizona/tuba-city.

ACCESS Physically challenged individuals will have difficulties negotiating the area in and around the dinosaur tracks. The ground is rough and uneven and there are large sandy areas. With some assistance, there are viewing areas where one can view the tracks from a distance.

NOTES I had a lot of fun here. I had done my homework in advance and knew what to expect. With that knowledge in hand, I found my travels throughout the tracksite enjoyable, refreshing and insightful. Sure, I got lots of misinformation and several tall tales, but that didn't diminish the awe I had of these prehistoric prints.

There are no hard and fast rules on how much you should give your tour guide. Remember that for many of the guides, this may be their only form of employment. This is Navajo and Hopi tribal land and you have been invited as a guest to see something few people will ever experience. Be sure to provide your guide with an appropriate amount of money and let him or her know how grateful you are for the time and information. Please don't be rude and stiff your guide just because all the facts weren't absolutely scientific or perfectly correct. Enjoy the journey.

That said, this is a venture well worth your time. If you've never seen dinosaur prints, this is the place to see them. As you look out over this incredible landscape, you can almost imagine herds (we're still not sure what to call a large group of dinosaurs) lumbering across a vast and muddy area. This is a site for those with lots of imagination and lots of creativity.

CHAPTER 13

Painted and Petrified Perspectives

One of the joys of paleontological research is the opportunity to meet some pretty incredible people—folks like Bill Parker.

"*Chindesaurus* truly represents the dawn of the dinosaurs—because it is actually one of the earliest dinosaurs," paleontologist Parker says about this mysterious and little-known creature. "And, when you look ahead into the Jurassic and the Cretaceous and see what dinosaurs become and look out your window today and see birds, which are living

The Petrified Forest is a place that amazes, delights, and fascinates.

dinosaurs, you're seeing that entire lineage that goes all the way back to dinosaurs such as *Chindesaurus*."

The Triassic Period is well represented by fossils discovered in the Petrified Forest.

I was sufficiently fascinated about dinosaurs of the Triassic period to chase after this enigmatic genus right where it lived . . . and died. I had made arrangements to interview Parker, who for the past decade has served as the park paleontologist at the Petrified Forest National Park in northeastern Arizona. He also maintains an unofficial blog (http://chinleana.blogspot.com/): his own personal discussion of Late Triassic paleontology and other assorted topics.

▲▼▲▼▲

I arrive at the park's visitor center on a typically sweltering late summer afternoon. Cars with license plates from Illinois, Wisconsin, Idaho, Ohio, and New Hampshire, and a host of Canadian provinces crowd the so-hot-you-could-fry-an-egg parking lot. I weave my way through the tourists buying postcards, authentic plastic dinosaurs, T-shirts, and other knickknacks. In short order, Bill comes down from his upstairs office.

Bill Parker looks every bit the part of a National Park Service ranger. Short brown hair, a pressed uniform with the requisite number of badges, and a trim muscular build make him the ideal recruiting tool for the park service. After an exchange of pleasantries, he asks if I'd like to see some prehistoric specimens in the back—an area of the park typically not open to tourists.

We weave our way into one of the back rooms, where he proudly shows me a collection of phytosaur fossils laid out on the shelves of a towering bookcase. We wedge ourselves between some cases and long filing cabinets and Bill slowly pulls out several drawers to display some of the other fossils discovered at the park over the years. He is like a father showing off all the photographs of all his babies—except that these babies have been around for far longer than any human types.

With the look of a Cheshire cat, he asks if I'd like to see the holotype (which in paleontology-speak usually means the first significant specimen found) of *Chindesaurus*. We weave back through the collection rooms to a metal cabinet measuring about 4 feet square. I sign my name on an official log book as Bill unlocks the case. Slowly and patiently he pulls out one of the drawers and there before me is the mother lode of Triassic fossils—the bones of *Chindesaurus*. Bill explains and demonstrates selected bones, my camera snapping away. With all the caution of a neurosurgeon, Bill carefully lifts selected pieces of the holotype out of the drawer and describes each one for me. His emotions are clearly evident—this is his pride and joy. I, too, am literally shaking with excitement!

After this 10-minute prehistoric show-and-tell (a singular and eye-popping experience in its own right) we retreat upstairs to Bill's tiny office, where his desk groans under the weight of research reports, monographs, administrative duties, and enough paperwork to sink a fleet of battleships. A small table is equally layered with papers and assignments, and the floor is a checkerboard of random piles of books, magazines, and paper. An omnipresent fan perched overhead keeps the stifling summer air moving around—barely.

As is often typical with many paleontologists, Bill came to his vocation in a roundabout way. "Like most six-year-olds I was interested in dinosaurs, prehistoric animals, and then I went my own way. You grow out of it. I ended up working in kitchens and restaurants and places like that. I worked my way up to management positions and decided that I didn't want to spend my life making someone else wealthy, that I was going to go back to school. And about that time, my mother bought me for my birthday, for some strange reason, a dinosaur calendar, 15 years after the fact. Things had changed a little in that time—dinosaurs weren't the sluggish beasts I remembered from my childhood. I was intrigued by that and so I bought a couple of books, started to get more interested, and then enrolled in geology classes in the local community college—Mesa Community College in Mesa, Arizona. I really enjoyed the professor that I had and became hooked on fossils."

I smiled at the reference to the professorial influence.

"How I ended up becoming a professional paleontologist is, right before I started my graduate degree from Northern Arizona University, I was volunteering at the Museum of Northern Arizona that, if you like fossils, a museum is the mandatory place to be, whether you get paid there or not. And I had just found out about a position working for the Forest Service, inventorying fossil localities, using historic photographs, historic records of collected fossils—you would go relocate the sites, redocument them using GPS, photography . . . this was in 1999. After about two years of that I ended up finding out about the job here— which was the same thing, another inventory position and got this one, and I'm still here—nine years later."

If ever there was a job for a nine-year-old boy cleverly disguised as an adult in a national park ranger uniform, this was it. The opportunity to get paid to explore your childhood passion must certainly be the epitome of pipe dreams.

But it was when I asked him what he liked or what intrigued him most about the field that his eyes began to sparkle, a devilish smile etched the corners of his mouth, and he sat up a little straighter in his chair. I had struck every interviewer's dream, the sine qua non of questions.

"What I like is figuring stuff out. I'm what you could call a 'historical' paleontologist. I like the idea that others have done this before me and like to go back and pore through their diaries and retrace their steps and find their old localities. That's what I really enjoy doing. I also just like solving problems. For example, a lot of these specimens are the only known from one skeleton—they're not complete. Trying to do the comparative work, the detective work, to figure out what these things were actually like . . . how they compare with each other—to me, I find that a lot of fun. For me that really pays off. It really gets in your blood. You're constantly trying to figure stuff out."

Bill elaborates on what any good paleontologist should have. "To be in this field, you have to have that drive—always trying to figure things out. For some people, paleontology is about big dinosaurs and they just like the idea of the whole adventure—all the *Jurassic Park* aspects—then they realize that it's a lot of work: Paleontology can be extremely difficult and frustrating; however, I actually get more encouraged by this difficulty 'cause I like figuring stuff out. When I run into a roadblock, I try to find out more information to work around that block."

The excitement in Bill's voice makes clear that here is someone in love with his job, but equally important, also with the possibilities his job entails. Bill is clearly passionate about what he doesn't know—what may be around the next corner or far into the future. It's not what he's learned that excites him so much, but what he may yet discover.

His work is clearly more than just an impersonal job description propagated by the park service. "My job is to manage the paleontological resources of this park, which means, as far as the vertebrate fossils go, that they aren't being eroded away, being lost, being stolen, being vandalized. I spend a lot of my time out in the field, looking for fossils, because they are slowly eroding out of the mud and hills out there and if I don't find them they'll be completely destroyed. After we collect them, we figure them out—how they go back together, what animals they represent. Sometimes we find new species that we get to name.

"I try to publish everything that we do in scientific journals that are widely accessible, rather than putting everything in an internal report that just goes into a file cabinet," he says proudly. "I also have a blog, as you know—the blog is not an official park service blog, but still covers Triassic paleontology." His enthusiasm escalates as he says, "So for our job, we go out and make sure no fossils are getting lost, care for the ones that we collect, and research the ones we collect; the information we determine gets passed on to our visitors and the scientific community."

The fan perched on the wall behind Bill is struggling to circulate the midsummer air in the cramped office. I'm eager to get his spin on *Chindesaurus,* certainly one of the park's proudest discoveries.

Chindesaurus (meaning "ghost lizard" or "spirit lizard," from the Navajo word *chindii*) is a genus of theropod dinosaur discovered in 1984 in the Painted Desert portion of the Petrified Forest National Park by Bryan Small. Its full name—*Chindesaurus bryansmalli*—actually means the "ghost lizard of Bryan Small."

Some of my preliminary research revealed that at the time of its discovery, *Chindesaurus* was erroneously billed in the media as the "world's earliest dinosaur." However, we now know it to be "*one* of the earliest dinosaurs." It was a slim bipedal (two-footed) carnivore that lived around 225 million years ago, during the Late Triassic period, in what is now northern Arizona. It was between 6 and 12 feet long.

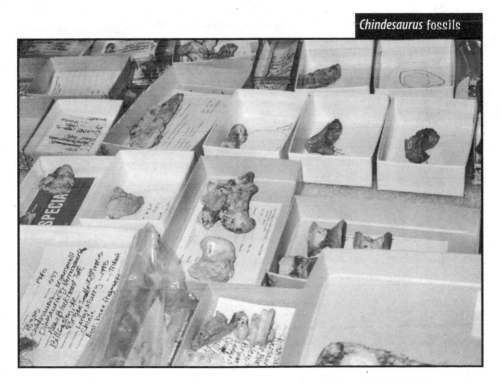
Chindesaurus fossils

Bill fills in some missing details. "*Chindesaurus* is important because when it was first collected, it was billed as the earliest dinosaur. There was a little bit of a misconception there—it wasn't the earliest dinosaur, time-wise. It was close . . . but there's stuff in Argentina that's actually older. But it was one of the most primitive dinosaurs found—that still stands today. There's a split in the dinosaur lineage between the bird-hipped dinosaurs and the lizard-hipped dinosaurs, and *Chindesaurus* is a member of the lizard-hipped, or saurischians, and one of the earliest known members of that group. In fact, that group, later on, splits into the theropod dinosaurs and the sauropods. *Chindesaurus* probably predates that split or is at the very beginning of one of those splits. It probably is a theropod.

"So," he continues, "*Chindesaurus* is more primitive than *Coelophysis,* which is the other well-known Triassic dinosaur. The prosauropods that are common in South America and Europe are also from the Triassic; however, they were unknown in North America at that time. In fact, the only thing comparable to *Chindesaurus,* what it's most closely related to, is a group of dinosaurs out of South America called herrerasaurs and these are the most primitive dinosaurs out there. Thus, *Chindesaurus* is a very primitive representative of the theropod (or meat-eating) dinosaurs in North America and the world."

One of the many fascinating aspects I am quickly learning about *Chindesaurus* is how much about it remains unknown. "What have we learned about *Chindesaurus* since its discovery?" I ask.

"When it was first collected, they thought from the ankle that it was a prosauropod—an ancestor of the big long-necked dinosaurs. Then for a while, the discoverers weren't so sure about that identification. Later on, it was contested whether it was even a dinosaur; at one time, it was thought that herrerasaurs were not true dinosaurs; rather, that they were ancestral to the dinosaurs. But now it's believed that they actually were dinosaurs—some of the oldest members of the theropods." Apparently, this is where *Chindesaurus* is fitting in right now, as an early dinosaur. "The holotype *Chindesaurus* is actually a key academic specimen in figuring a lot of these relationships out. Some of the elements such as the leg, ankle, and vertebrae are very well preserved."

Once again his eyes sparkle when I ask him what he personally considers to be the most amazing aspect about *Chindesaurus*. "For me, that we have primitive theropod dinosaurs in North America during the Triassic. Prior to the discovery of *Chindesaurus,* they were only known from South America. It shows that we have some of those early lineages here in North America." As before, his fascination with the unknown surfaces. "I'd like to find more of *Chindesaurus.* I'd like to know what the skull was like. I'd like to know what the pelvis was like. But the fact that we actually have some representatives of the earliest dinosaurs here is pretty sensational."

I'm curious about the fossils I saw in the cabinet in the paleontology laboratory, and their role in this process.

"I think it's important for people to realize that because of the limitations of the fossil record (preservation), we don't always find beautiful, perfect articulated skeletons," he says, "but that doesn't make the fossils any less important. Despite its being incomplete, we still have some key features preserved in *Chindesaurus* that tell us a lot about it. However, we're missing more than we know, such as the skull, arms, and so on. That makes us want to go out and find more of it. And the uncertainty is kind of a wide-open book.

"Who knows what we're going to learn about *Chindesaurus* when we find the rest of it? What the skull looks like? What the pelvis looks like? One of the great things about working in the Triassic is it was a real interesting time. There was a lot of experimentation going on. This is one of the reasons why I like the Triassic. There was a major extinction at the end of the Permian and the slate was pretty much wiped clean. And one of the groups that takes off afterward is the archeosaurs, which dinosaurs were a member of. By the time you get to the Jurassic and Cretaceous, everything's a dinosaur.

"But in the Triassic, there's this wonderful, experimental time where you have the crocodile-like guys, you have the dinosaurs—they're all

Ancient trees in the Petrified Forest National Park

doing the same thing—plus there are a lot of different body plans in other animal groups, things you don't see later on. So, working in the Triassic, you have the opportunity to find something completely new—I'm not talking about new species; I'm talking about completely new families. You actually have that possibility here."

By this point in our conversation, I'm ready to turn in my professor's hat and exchange it for a park service uniform and a shovel. I'm not sure if I'm being recruited or unduly influenced, but I'm ready to join the cause.

Bill continues, "The *Chindesaurus*, when we actually find the complete skeleton, may turn out to be something totally different from anything we've actually seen before. It might have no teeth, it might be beaked. I don't know—anything's possible with these things. It may have long, razor-sharp claws—we don't know. That's one of the really interesting things about the Triassic. Sometimes what you don't know about something is a lot more interesting than what you do know. We're going to keep going out there [into the park badlands] to find this thing. And one day, somebody will find the rest of it. And when they do, I'm sure it will be pretty amazing."

The Painted Desert and the Petrified Forest is rife with striking vistas, panoramic views, and stupendous landscapes that amaze, delight, and fascinate. This is a land of contrasts—a palette of colors and hues found nowhere else in the world—and one of exquisite beauty. And beneath the topography and visual sensations is an abundance of paleontological treasures waiting to be discovered.

"The Petrified Forest is important because it represents the best accessible exposures of the Chinle formation, which is the Late Triassic rock formation that fossils here occur in," Bill explains. "The Chinle formation is exposed from Utah all the way into Mexico, but in a lot of cases it's inaccessible—either because it's privately owned or because it's covered with vegetation or exposed in the side of a cliff. Here, we get nice three-dimensional exposures—they aren't covered with vegetation. Because it's a national park, they're accessible to researchers—one of the mandates of the National Park Service is to foster and encourage research, which is another big part of my job. This park is a window through which we can view the Triassic period, a window that we don't have in a lot of other places . . . and here is one the best accessible places on Earth to study it."

"So, the Painted Desert and Petrified Forest involve a lot of paleontology?" I query.

Bill nods. "I'd like to reiterate about the purpose of the park service," he says. We're here to facilitate research and generate additional information to the public. That's the whole purpose of the park service. We're here to protect the fossils and to disseminate the information about them to the public."

Bill smiles and totally agrees with my overall assessment of our conversation: that his job is the best of two worlds—one past and one present.

NEED TO KNOW

DIRECTIONS From Flagstaff head east on I-40 to Holbrook (about 91 miles). Take exit 285 to US 180 E and drive for about 19 miles to the south entrance of the park. Drive north in the park to I-40.

From Flagstaff, the drive is about 110 miles and will take you about 2 1/2 hours.

CONTACT INFORMATION **Petrified Forest National Park**, P.O. Box 2217, Petrified Forest, AZ 86028 (928-524-6228; www.nps.gov/pefo).

FEES Private vehicles $10; single bicyclists, motorcyclists, and walk-ins $5.

HOURS Different hours are observed at various times of the year—mostly 7 AM–6 PM. Check the website for specific hours for the time of year you are planning to visit.

BEST TIME TO VISIT Any time during the year except December 25, when the park is closed.

CAMPING/LODGING There are no campgrounds in the park. However there is plenty of lodging available in nearby Holbrook ("Gateway to the Petrified Forest National Park"). There are 16 hotels/motels (mostly

the major chains) and two RV parks in town. You can get the latest information and phone numbers at www.ci.holbrook.az.us.

ACCESS All park buildings are handicapped accessible.

NOTES This national park is a must-see. Although you won't see any dinosaur fossils here, you will get a sense of the Triassic environment in which several dinosaurs lived, while being able to drive through an incredible landscape filled with color, artistry, and prehistory. You can easily zip through the park in an hour or spend the entire day here, exploring and visiting sites you'll find nowhere else in the country.

The 28-mile park road offers overlooks with long-distance vistas of the Painted Desert and Petrified Forest. There are many parking areas with access to hiking trails, picnic areas, and the designated wilderness. Hiking trails range from the very easy 0.4-mile paved Giant Logs Trail to the strenuous and steep 1-mile loop Blue Mesa Trail. Most trails are easy and relatively short.

Part of the Chinle formation in southeastern Utah

CHAPTER 14

Of Names and *Sonorasaurus*

Names.

We all have them. Some of us really like our names and others seriously question what our parents were thinking when they gave us a name that is either too difficult for most people to pronounce or so silly that it evokes laughter—particularly when we're eight years old and trying to be cool with all our friends on the playground. Names are as much a part of who we are as are our personality quirks or physiological measurements.

Prickly pear cactus at the Arizona–Sonora Desert Museum

Until I began writing this chapter, I didn't know there was a science of names. In fact, that science is called onomastics (from the Greek *onoma,* which means "name"). Onomasticians (yes, it's a real word) are folks who spend their career looking into the etymology, or origin, of given names,[22] how names are used in various cultures, and why some are chosen more often by parents than are others. The etymology of names is the study of the origin and literal meaning of names. For example, my

22   A given name is a (first) name that is assumed by a person at or immediately after birth. This is in opposition to a family name (e.g., Smith, Jones, Doe); a given name is generally not inherited. In Europe and North America, where the given name precedes the family name, given names are called first names or forenames. They are sometimes referred to as Christian names.

first name—Anthony—is an English form of the Roman family name Antonius, which is of unknown Etruscan origin. In short, my name has no specific meaning (although I'm sure my parents thought otherwise). On the other hand, my wife's name—Phyllis—means "foliage" in Greek—in Greek mythology, this was the name of a woman who killed herself out of love for Demophon and was subsequently transformed into an almond tree.

Well, just imagine if you or somebody else discovered a long-lost dinosaur and somebody went and named it after you. That, you must admit, would be quite interesting.

Well, that's just what happened a few years ago. So let's take a little journey to southeastern Arizona, where I'd like to introduce you to a most remarkable creature (actually two remarkable creatures) from a most remarkable place.

▲▼▲▼▲

During the Cretaceous period, many parts of what was to become Arizona were relatively flat and the climate was hot, wet, and humid. Southern Arizona, for example, had a most interesting variety of dinosaurs during this time. Carnivorous dinosaurs wandered the edges of the marshy ecosystem, looking for prey, while herbivorous dinosaurs feasted on enormous spreads of cycads, ferns, and short conifers. It is likely that the bones of these prehistoric beasts were common; but, according to several paleontologists many of the resultant fossils were most likely destroyed through eons of volcanic activity and powerful geological forces.

During the autumn of 1994, amateur fossil collector Richard Thompson was exploring the rolling hills of southeastern Arizona near the very small town of Sonoita, looking for petrified logs. Because this region was punctuated by large forests in the Cretaceous period, petrified wood is a common fossil in what is now the Sonoran Desert. Thompson knew that fragments of dinosaur bone had also been found in this region, but that they were extremely rare. Nevertheless, as he wandered about he kept his eyes open for fossilized materials of any type—plants or animals.

And, then, there it was!

In the cliff face of a remote canyon, jutting out of the hard Cretaceous sandstone of 100 million years ago, were fossilized bones too big to be from anything other than a dinosaur.

Thompson's chance find turned out to be the first glimpse of a 51-foot-long dinosaur—later named *Sonorasaurus* (Sonoran

Sonorasaurus had 12-foot-long legs.

lizard)—that lived about 100 million years ago (middle Cretaceous period). By comparison, its length (51 feet long) and weight (40-50 tons) would be equivalent to a modern-day right whale. This dinosaur had a giraffe-like stance, a long neck, an equally long tail, a bulky body, and a small head. It was, and still is, the only dinosaur skeleton ever found in southern Arizona and the largest dinosaur found in all of Arizona.

It is speculated the dinosaur died in a forested environment and was washed into a narrow river. There, floodwaters and thousands of feet of sandstone eventually covered the carcass for millions of years until volcanic action uplifted the rocks and exposed the fossils.

After several test excavations at the site and visits to major dinosaur museums to compare bones, the staff at the Arizona–Sonora Desert determined that the fossils belonged to a brachiosaur, one of the largest dinosaurs ever to roam the Earth. More surprisingly, brachiosaurs—long-necked, long-tailed herbivores—were thought to have died out some 125 million years ago. Among the brachiosaurs were some of the largest creatures to have walked the Earth. Comparative measurements of the feet and limbs of *Sonorasaurus* initially indicated that this individual may have been a juvenile, a teenager as dinosaurs go, having fully adult-size feet while the rest of the body would still have been growing.

You can see an exhibit dedicated to *Sonorasaurus* at the Arizona–Sonora Desert Museum. As part of that display visitors can read about what life was like 100 million years ago in this part of the world. They can learn how *Sonorasaurus* died and how it was discovered. One part of the exhibit is a simulated rock face that shows exactly what Rich Thompson saw in 1994—specifically how the bones might have appeared if the surrounding rock could have been removed without disturbing them.[23] In addition, there is a replica of the right front leg of *Sonorasaurus* that, at least according to my measurements, is about 12 feet tall. A posted sign next to the leg states, "It is estimated this specimen measured 55 to 60 long and stood 15 feet high at the shoulder with a head and neck that reached 20 to 25 feet into the trees. It may have weighed as much as 40 tons."

For me, one of the most interesting aspects of this creature was how it may have died. According to the displays at the museum, "*Sonorasaurus*

Sonorasaurus bones on display at the Arizona–Sonora Desert Museum.

---

23 The "bones" in the exhibit are replicas made from molds that captured the exact shape and texture of the real *Sonorasaurus* bones. A map made during the actual excavation was used to guide bone placement in the exhibit. The original bones are stored in the museum's vault.

probably died in the bed of a shallow stream (there's ample sedimentary evidence that shows the carcass caused a large dam in the river channel as it lay there). After its death much of the skeleton was broken, either by being trodden upon by scavengers or rolled downstream by flowing water, eventually burying it. Over time, the remains were covered by a thick layer of mud. These sediments gradually hardened into stone that, eventually, was later tilted upright by geologic forces."

Most fascinating of all was the discovery of tooth marks on some of the bones. According to the museum, "These indicate that neighborhood carnivorous dinosaurs of the time may have scavenged on the *Sonorasaurus* carcass and carried off parts of the body. Equally interesting, was when a three-inch-long, serrated tooth, found near the bones, matched the scars on the *Sonorasaurus* bones. Those tooth gouges were later determined to be those of the carnivorous [and apparently opportunistic] *Acrocanthosaurus*."

The museum also contends, "*Acrocanthosaurus* [meaning 'high-spine lizard', is a reference to the extended row of 17-inch spikes growing out of its spine] was one of the largest and fiercest theropods of the Cretaceous. It was roughly 38 feet long and weighed in at a staggering seven tons. Nineteen serrated teeth lined each side of the upper jaw (the number of teeth in the lower jaw has not yet been determined). With its powerful arms, sickle-like claws on each hand, and predatory nature it would have been a fearsome killing machine—even for the much larger *Sonorasaurus*."

▲ ▼ ▲ ▼ ▲

Fascinated by the life, death, and discovery of *Sonorasaurus,* I contacted Rich Thompson to get his spin on this story. When I asked him to describe his personal history he said, "I was born while my father was at med school. After his residency, we returned to Tucson, where both my sets of grandparents lived. It was 1970; I was nine. I grew up here obsessed with all things natural, particularly snakes. I had gone through a serious dinosaur phase earlier, but I was then interested in things I could touch. I have always had a deep affinity for the desert. Later, I went to college for a while, then I dropped out Around 1991, someone lent me a copy of *Jurassic Park.* After I read it, I decided I should do some fossil hunting. So I learned how to read a geologic map, and I got a lot of help from the great guys at the Arizona Geological Society and from a retired paleontologist named Halsey Miller, who knows the area."

Rich told me that he was originally attracted to the area near Sonoita after reading some publications produced by the Arizona Geological Society. Those documents described the stratigraphy (a branch of geology focused on rock layers and layering, or stratification) of the region and mentioned some crumbling bone chips. He then started exploring the area, first with his girlfriend's brother, and then with another friend. As he says, "It was obvious from some of the float that no one had really gone over the area."

What Rich Thompson may have seen back in 1994

Are The Dinosaur Bones In This Rock?

When I asked how he knew he had discovered something unusual, he told me, "I was walking the bases of ridges, looking for bone chip trails. I found one with some big chunks in it. It started and stopped off and on up the ridge. For the last twenty feet or so below the crest of the ridge, there were no chips, but I knew from the quantity of float that something good had to be nearby. In this area, the layers are nearly vertical, and last few feet of the ridge were an exposed bedding plane of sandstone."

As is often the case in paleontology, Lady Luck stepped in. Rich explains, "Finally, I just looked at the rock and a piece of scapula (shoulder blade) bigger than my head was exposed. Right next to it, cross-sections of three ribs were sticking out. A quick inspection showed other bones sticking out. It was obvious it was a good one. And since late Cretaceous [dinosaurs] were then, and still to some extent are not, that well known and certainly not from here, it was likely to be interesting."

Interesting! Perhaps that's putting it mildly. Just imagine how "interesting" it would be to find a chest of buried treasure in your backyard while barbecuing hamburgers on a summer afternoon.

"Right about then," Rich related, "I thought I was having a coronary. I started shaking and climbed on top of the ridge and started yelling, 'I've made a mega-find.' I'm just glad the shock didn't kill me."

I was curious as to what Rich thought was the most amazing or memorable thing about the discovery. He said, "Just seeing one bone after another sticking out of the rock!"

Since that unbelievable discovery, Rich has been to the area many times, but not for the purpose of finding fossils. He's a fan of the desert and simply enjoys hiking through this remote area.

▲▼▲▼▲

Okay, so now we have this brand-new dinosaur—the only one ever discovered in southeastern Arizona. It's unusual, it's distinctive, and it's unique. And, like you and me, it needed a name—a full and proper name. So let's return to our discussion of names.

Paleontologists want to be sure that the names they give to organisms—particularly dead organisms—are both exact and precise. (There's no sense having two different creatures both with the same name.) Therefore, there are some rules that they follow.

You know how some kind of governmental group, regulatory agency, commission, or group always wants to tell you how to do something— someone telling you when to pay your taxes, that you need a license, how to build according to code, when you need a passport, and so on. Well, scientists have their own regulatory agency telling them what to do (surprise!)—particularly when they want to name an animal, especially an animal that's been dead for a long time (think dinosaurs).

This agency is the International Code of Zoological Nomenclature (ICZN), which governs the creation of scientific names of all animals, dinosaurs included. The ICZN specifies that each animal must have a two-part scientific name (often in Latin) that is the same throughout the world. The first, more general part of any scientific name is the genus to which the organism belongs. A genus is a group of one or more closely related species thought to have evolved from a common ancestor and sharing many unique characters.

The second part of a scientific name is the species name. A species is a group of organisms that breed naturally with one another and do not breed with other such groups (species). Just so you're perfectly clear on the naming of dinosaurs, the ICZN states that "a generic name must be a singular Latin noun in nominative case and that the species epithet must be linguistically constructed as a modifier of that noun." Got that?

For example, here are the scientific names of some critters with whom you may be more familiar:

Cat:	*Felis catus*
Pig:	*Sus domestica*
Robin:	*Turdus migratorius*

Giraffe: *Giraffa camelopardalis*[24]

Great white shark: *Carcharodon carcharias*

In most cases, dinosaurs are named by the people who discover them. Or they are given names by the paleontologist or paleontologists who publish the discovery in a recognized professional journal. In short, whoever finds a dinosaur, or writes about it first, gets to assign the name. Now, to you and me it often seems as if dinosaur names are complicated strings of letters designed to test either our pronunciation abilities or linguistic prowess, or both. In actuality, dinosaur names are usually combinations of word roots that have some sort of special meaning—especially for the person doing the naming. For example, *Triceratops* is a combination of three descriptive word roots: *tri-* (from the Latin, meaning "three"); *cerat-* (from the Greek, meaning "horn"); and *-ops* (from the Greek, meaning "face"). Thus, we have a dinosaur with a three-horned face.

Another Southwestern dinosaur, *Pachycephalosaurus*, is also a combination of three word roots: *pachy-* (from the Greek, meaning "thick"); *cephalo-* (from the Greek, meaning "head"); and *-saurus* (from the Greek, meaning "lizard"). While you may think that this name ("thick-headed-lizard") is a reflection of the creature's overall intelligence, such is not the case. The name actually describes an animal with a projection on the upper part of the skull, making the head look thicker than normal.

The first scientifically named dinosaur genus (in 1824) was *Megalosaurus*.

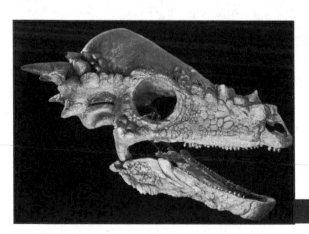

Skull of *Pachycephalosaurus*

---

24 In the 14th century, Europeans believed that these creatures were a cross between a camel and a leopard (they were known as "camelopards"). The modern-day species name is derived from that antiquated belief.

It was constructed by Reverend William Buckland from the Greco-Latin root *saurus* ("lizard") and the Greek *megas* ("great"). Since then, *saurus* has been the most popular ending for a dinosaur name (e.g., *Tyrannosaurus*, *Apatosaurus*). *Odon* (Latinized Greek for "tooth") is the second most popular ending for a dinosaur name (e.g., *Troodon*, *Deinodon*).

For the sake of consistency, the first name (the genus) of a newly discovered dinosaur is often, but not always, a combination of one or more Latin and/or Greek word roots. Here is a list of word roots commonly used in dinosaur names.

Word Root	Meaning	Word Root	Meaning
allo	other or different	ichthyo	fish
anato	duck	lopho	ridged
ankylo	crooked	mega	large
anuro	tail	metro	measured
apato	deceptive	micro	small
avi	bird	nycho	clawed
bary	heavy	pachy	thick
brachio	arm	para	beside
bronto	thunder	pod, ped	foot
cera	horned	proto	first
caudia	tail	raptor	thief
cephalo	head	rex	king
chasmo	opening	saurus	lizard
coeli	hollow	stego	roof
compso	pretty	steno	slender
diplo	two	super	superior
dino	terrible	thero	beast
docus	beam	tri	three
don	tooth	tyranno	tyrant
elasmo	plated	ultra	extreme
gnathus	jaw	urus	tail
hadro	large	veloci	speedy

Here are a few dinosaurs with names you don't hear very often:

Oviraptor: "egg eater"

Psittacosaurus: "parrot-reptile"

Avimimus: "bird mimic"

Ornitholestes: "bird robber"

Heterodontosaurus: "reptile with different-size teeth"

Ankylosaurus: "fused reptile"

Dinosaur names can also describe where the animal was first discovered. For example, *Albertosaurus* was discovered in the province of Alberta, Canada; *Minmi* was discovered near Minmi Crossing in Australia; *Argentinosaurus* was discovered in Argentina; and *Bactrosaurus* was discovered in Bactria, Mongolia.

Model of *Psittacosaurus*

Quite often, dinosaur names honor the person who was instrumental in the discovery. As an example, *Lambeosaurus* was named for Lawrence Lambe, a paleontologist with the Geological Survey of Canada; *Laellynasaura* was named for a little girl, Laellyn Rich, who asked her parents to find her a dinosaur; and *Diplodocus carnegii* was named for Andrew Carnegie, who financed the expedition for its discovery.

Skeleton of *Lambeosaurus*

Interestingly, dinosaurs have been named for almost everything under the sun. They've been named for specific parts of their anatomy, for their lifestyles, and for some of the foods they consumed. They've been named for mythological creatures, heavenly bodies, military armaments, corporations, and ancient civilizations. They've also been named for geographical features, as well as countries, cities, and states. Here are a few examples:

Camelotia:	"of Camelot"
Harpymimus:	"harpy [a mythological bird] mimic"
Lophorhothon:	"crested nose"
Malawisaurus:	"Malawi lizard"
Opisthocoelicaudia:	"behind Hollow Tail"
Pawpawsaurus:	"Paw Paw [from the eastern Texas Paw Paw rock formation] lizard"
Tarchia:	"brainy"
Technosaurus:	"Texas Tech University lizard"
Utahraptor:	"Utah lizard"
Volkheimeria:	"Volkheimer's lizard"

▲▼▲▼▲

Now, let's return to our friend *Sonorasaurus*. Because this dinosaur was found in a part of the Sonoran Desert called the Chihuahua Desert, Ronald Ratkevich, a paleontologist at the Arizona–Sonora Desert Museum, at first wanted to name the dinosaur *Chihuahuasaurus*, but felt the name might not be appropriate for a 51-foot-long animal. However, as you will recall, *Sonorasaurus* was discovered in the Sonoran Desert by Richard Thompson. Using all the rules and regulations and requirements above, it seemed only fitting to give it the most logical name of all— *Sonorasaurus thompsoni* ("Thompson's Sonoran Desert lizard").

So, if you're looking for a little immortality while you're still alive, go out and discover a new dinosaur. People will talk about you (or your name) for years!

NEED TO KNOW

DIRECTIONS From Tucson: *Eastbound:* exit I-10 at Speedway Blvd and turn right. After 12 miles, turn right onto Kinney Road. In about 2.5 miles, the Desert Museum will be on your left. *Westbound:* exit I-10 at 29th Street, take the frontage road north to Speedway Blvd and turn left. After 12 miles, turn right onto Kinney Road. In about 2.5 miles, the Desert Museum will be on your left.

CONTACT INFORMATION **Arizona–Sonora Desert Museum**, 2021 N. Kinney Rd., Tucson, AZ 85743 (520-883-2702; www.desertmuseum. org).

FEES Sept.–May: adults $14.50, children 6–12 $4.50; June–Aug.: adults $12, children 6–12 $3, children 5 and under free.

HOURS Oct.–Feb. 8:30–5 (no entry after 4:15 PM), Mar.–May 7:30–5 (no entry after 4:15 PM); June–Aug. Sun.–Fri. 7–4:30 (no entry after 3:45 PM), Sat. 7 AM–10 PM (no entry after 9:15 PM); Sept. 7–4:30 (no entry after 3:45 PM).

BEST TIME TO VISIT The Arizona–Sonora Desert Museum is open every day of the year. *However,* if you visit during the summer and don't slather lots of sunscreen on your skin, or wear a hat and sunglasses, then you'll be sorry! Also, as the museum is primarily an outdoor experience, you need to keep the outside temperature in mind when planning a visit. That said, you should know that all indoor exhibits are cooled for your comfort. (My first visit was in late July, and by preparing ahead of time, I had a very comfortable day-long journey throughout the grounds while the outside temperature never dipped below the triple digits. Of course, I also went through about 8,693 gallons of drinking water.)

CAMPING/LODGING There are thousands of places to stay while you're in the Tucson area. You can find the best information about available lodging at the website for the Metropolitan Tucson Convention and Visitor's Bureau (www.visittucson.org). Here you'll be able to see all the resorts, spas, hotels, guest ranches, B&Bs, vacation packages, and vacation rentals in the area—everything from ultra-cheap to ultra-expensive (and lots in between).

ACCESS All parts of the museum grounds are wheelchair accessible. Motorized scooters can also be rented for a nominal fee.

NOTES The Arizona–Sonora Desert Museum describes itself as "a world-renowned zoo, natural history museum and botanical garden, all in one place." Spend a day walking around the grounds and you'll encounter an incredible assembly of plants and animals native to a desert environment. Best of all, the critters are all displayed in natural settings (several even roaming free). The entire museum encompasses 21 acres of land and enough outdoor paths for the heartiest of walkers.

Shortly after you pass through the museum entrance and head along the path to your right you will come upon the Earth Sciences Center. Here you will discover several displays and lots of information about *Sonorasaurus* and its discovery. Kids can stand next to one of the dinosaur's leg bones as well as a replica of how its bones were first seen by Richard Thompson (you may want to read this chapter in advance of your visit, to put this section of the museum into proper perspective).

This is truly one of the best museums in the entire country—a one-of-a-kind destination that will keep the kids engaged and the adults informed. It's also one of those places where it is almost impossible to see everything in a single visit. You'll need to plan your time here carefully (be sure to get one of the self-guided tour maps). Whatever you do, be sure to put this unique experience on your travel plans—you will not regret it! Be sure to check out the museum's excellent website, which has tons of information to help you plan your visit.

The Dinosaur on My Desk

On the shelf behind my computer is a twelve-piece, three-dimensional wooden puzzle. It is a dinosaur puzzle my son gave me a few Christmases ago. I'm not quite sure what type of dinosaur it is, but with its stout body, short neck, fat tail, and sizable head it looks something like a macabre cross between a *Ceolophysis* on steroids and an *Apatosaurus* in the last stages of the Ironman Triathlon . . . in other words, it's a puzzle! It is divided into several interlocking pieces all carefully crafted and all carefully assembled into a complex prehistoric pattern. The "Ceolo-saurus" regularly glares at me with a decidedly

Dinosaurs offer many intriguing puzzles for paleontologists, tourists, and authors.

defiant attitude—one I fear is a not-so-subtle challenge to take it down, take it apart, and consume the better part of a rainy afternoon trying to put back together again. I suppose it's not too much of a stretch to see this dinosaur puzzle as a metaphor for the mysteries, conundrums, enigmas, riddles, and challenges of Southwestern paleontology.

In some ways this book was a way to link my childhood passion for things prehistoric with my innate, and still growing, sense of adventure. Time after time, I realized that, as in most educational journeys, it wasn't the answers that were the most important element, but the processes employed to seek the answers (or as the great philosophers would say, "The journey is more important than the destination."). For me, as I hope it was for you, this book was a journey of body and mind . . . as well as heart and soul. Sure, the answers were significant, but the chance

to create learning opportunities and walk in the shoes of professional paleontologists through the soaring mesas, rock-ribbed canyons, and long pebbled deserts of the Southwest may be the most significant part of this educational adventure.

Like the feline who continually experiments with each of its nine lives, I've always had this insatiable curiosity. I've frequently enjoyed posing questions for which I have no idea of the response—and then going out and seeking an answer. I'm fond of discovering topics that have little to do with my career as a professor of education, but that provide me with a broad range of experiences I might not otherwise consider. For me, as I hope it is for you, life is a constant series of intellectual experiences—looking around the corner, peeking at distant sites, and gazing at the incredible.

For our dinosaurian queries we've traveled to locations in both Arizona and New Mexico—places that held as many answers as they did puzzles. Together, we've discovered, not only the data and tales surrounding some incredible creatures, but the places where these critters walked, slept, and preyed on one another—ever since the beginning of time (or, at least, the beginning of the Triassic period). We've generated questions and immersed ourselves in a host of scientific pursuits throughout the Southwest. We've become fellow paleo-adventurers who sought answers to perplexing prehistoric queries. We sought new territories and new adventures—places where stories and secrets were waiting to be uncovered by those of us with a passion for discovery. Together, we probed the unknown and peeked into the past.

Bill Parker, the paleontologist at Petrified Forest National Park in Arizona, said it best when he told me, "It really gets in your blood. You're constantly trying to figure stuff out. To be in this field you have to have that drive—*always trying to figure things out.*"

I hope you've enjoyed this journey—this prehistoric puzzle of both time and place. I also hope that, like me, you've discovered a few answers along the way.

Selected Reading

Colbert, Edwin H. *The Great Dinosaur Hunters and Their Discoveries*. New York: Dover Publications, 1984.

This book takes you inside the lives of the men and (very few) women who blazed paleontological trails across the American West and around the world with their discoveries and explorations. This is the human side of the world of dinosaurs—and a most readable side it is.

Foster, John. *Jurassic West: The Dinosaurs of the Morrison Formation and Their World*. Bloomington, Indiana: Indiana University Press, 2007.

Throughout the American Southwest, the Morrison Formation has given up some of the most compelling information about dinosaurs. Written by an eminent paleontologist, this is the story of life in an ancient world that continues to amaze and confound.

Fredericks, Anthony D. *Walking with Dinosaurs: Rediscovering Colorado's Prehistoric Beasts*. Boulder, CO: Johnson Books, 2012.

With a liberal dose of humor and a sense of adventure, the author takes readers to various dinosaur digs throughout Colorado to explore the prehistoric past. Colorado has more dinosaurs than any other state and this book takes readers to all the places where they now reside—permanently.

Horner, Jack, and Gorman, James. *How to Build a Dinosaur: Extinction Doesn't Have to be Forever*. New York: Dutton, 2009.

Noted paleontologist Jack Horner and his colleagues in molecular biology labs are prepared to create a *real* dinosaur based on the latest breakthroughs—without using prehistoric DNA. Horner outlines a plan to "reverse evolution" and reveals an awesome plan to re-create the prehistoric past.

Johnson, Kirk, and Troll, Ray. *Cruisin' the Fossil Freeway.* Golden, CO: Fulcrum Publishing, 2007.

This is the story of a delightful journey across the American Southwest by a paleontologist and an artist in their never-ending search for fossils. There are adventures galore, sights to see, and an infectious sense of humor that will keep readers enthralled to the very end.

Long, John. *Feathered Dinosaurs: The Origin of Birds.* London: Oxford University Press, 2008.

This paleontologist provides a stunning visual record of these extraordinary prehistoric creatures, illuminating the evolutionary march from primitive, feathered dinosaurs through to the first true flying birds. This book provides a compelling and convincing argument for the bird-dinosaur connection.

Manning, Philip. *Grave Secrets of Dinosaurs: Soft Tissues and Hard Science.* Washington, D.C.: National Geographic Society, 2008.

In 1997, a high school student discovers a nearly complete dinosaur mummy. This sets off a chain of events that would rival any detective yarn. This book reads like a novel but is packed with more science than you can shake a stick at. It is a difficult book to put down.

Mitchell, W. J. T. *The Last Dinosaur Book.* University of Chicago: Chicago Press, 1988.

This author, an eminent cultural historian, puts dinosaurs in their proper place, both as sociological icons and as scientific curiosities, in this heavy though very informative book. In 320 pages, he answers the pervasive question, "Why are dinosaurs so popular?"

Parker, Steve, and Mertz, Leslie. *Extreme Dinosaurs.* New York: Collins, 2008.

This is a very readable and thorough examination of the Age of

Dinosaurs. Each of the chapters is brief, but chock-full of interesting facts and incredible data. This is a must-have for any dinophile!

Paul, Gregory. *The Scientific American Book of Dinosaurs*. New York: St. Martin's Griffin, 2003.

This book provides a complete portrait of dinosaurs' existence, including how they evolved, what they looked like, where they lived, how they behaved, and why they died. The most sensational finds and the latest theories are covered in this comprehensive tome.

Acknowledgments

This book would not have been possible without the guidance, support, professionalism, encouragement, and enthusiasm of many people (and one cat)—all of whom embraced this work and offered immeasurable words of wisdom.

I want to thank Amy Henrici at the Carnegie Museum of Natural History, who shared the demands of paleontological field work and the intricacies of fossil preparation. Thanks also to Dennis Brownridge of the Orme School, who gave me a quick course in Southwestern geology and a gentle reminder about the value of a Southwestern education.

I am particularly grateful to several individuals who allowed me to top into their brain power to better understand the dinosaurs of the desert. Richard Thompson offered a rich and interesting history of *Sonorasaurus*, and Tom Williamson of the New Mexico Museum of Natural History and Science proffered delightful insights about the "Bisti Beast." I am especially thankful to Bill Parker of the Painted Desert National Park, who willingly shared his passion and perspectives on little known aspects of the Triassic period—especially *Chindesaurus*.

Frank Faustine and all the blue-vested volunteers at the New Mexico Museum of Natural History and Science deserve high fives and a standing ovation for their knowledge, graciousness, and all-around attention to customer service. They make a visit to this world-class museum an educational experience second to none.

My travels through Arizona would not have been complete without the incredible day I spent with Mesach outside Tuba City. He was fun to be with and made an otherwise sweltering day both delightful and memorable!

The folks at The Countryman Press are an absolute joy to work with. They are a class act in the publishing business and their skill and attention to detail are without equal, without parallel. Many thanks to my editorial director, Kermit Hummel, and photo editor, Caitlin

Martin, for their constant communiqués, unmitigated support, and overwhelming enthusiasm for this project.

Ultimately, this book would not be what it is without the eagle eyes and editorial hand-holding of my copy editor, Iris Bass. That you are able to read and enjoy this book without tripping over dangling modifiers, stumbling over non sequiturs, or weaving your way through disjointed verbiage is due to her tireless efforts on my behalf. Iris is a nonfiction author in her own right and she knows the species well. "Thanks" hardly seems appropriate for her numerous contributions to this project.

Finally, my undying appreciation goes to my constant morning companion (and all-around supercat)—Tubby. An audience of one, his presence beneath my desk each day allowed me to vent (when something wasn't working) and sing (when things were "clicking"). The fact that he slept through most of the process is completely immaterial.

Tony Fredericks

Contact Me

I would like to hear from you—especially if you enjoyed visiting a place featured in this book. I'd also like to know if something did not work out for you as you had hoped. If you have suggestions for other sites or locations for future editions of this book, please contact me. I would truly value your experiences, your journeys, and your ideas. You are welcome to contact me through the publisher or directly (afredericks60@comcast.net).

If you would like information on other books I've written (children's books, teacher books, trade books) please log my name (Anthony D. Fredericks) into the appropriate author spaces on Amazon.com or Barnes & Noble.com. New titles are added each year.

Index:

Dinosaurs discussed in this book